THE SOUL'S PROGRESS

A Time for All Seasons

Lisa Saddler

To Vinnie,
Who understands
from the author
Time + Conway
Lisa Saddler
April 1999

ANAIIS PRESS

Copyright © 1999 by Lisa Saddler

All rights reserved. This book, or parts thereof, may not be reproduced in any form without written permission.

Library of Congress Cataloging-in-Publication Data: 98-95029
Saddler, Lisa
    The Soul's Progress / Lisa Saddler
      p, cm.
    ISBN: 0-9670033-0-X
    1. Soul   2. Psychic   3. Extrasensory perception
    3. Supernatural
    I. Title

Grateful acknowledgment is made for permission to reprint from:
PSI, What is it? Louisa E. Rhine, copyright © 1975, HarperCollins Publishers.

Cover photograph by Anne A. Conway
Cover graphics by Barbara Allie

Printed in the United States

THE SOUL'S PROGRESS

A Time for All Seasons

In memory of my loved ones

for

Marcus, Andrea, Griffin, Scott, Madeline

Calpurnia here, my wife, stays me at home.

She dreamt tonight she saw my statue,

Which like a fountain with an hundred spouts

Did run pure blood; and many lusty Romans

Came smiling, and did bathe their hands in it.

And these does she apply for warnings and portents

And evils imminent; and on her knee

Hath begged that I will stay at home today.

Julius Caesar

Contents

Introduction

1. *The Cosmos' Call* — 1
2. *The Sun also Sets* — 19
3. *On a Clear Day* — 32
4. *Across the Horizon* — 45
5. *Other Places* — 60
6. *Adrift* — 75
7. *Crossings* — 85
8. *The Soul's Embrace* — 92
9. *Unto the Fold* — 104
10. *From this Day* — 113
11. *Shadows of the Moonlight* — 126
12. *Gentle Healings* — 145
13. *Transitions* — 160
14. *All Seasons* — 172

Epilogue - The Quest — 184

Q & A — 201

Glossary — 213

Author's Note

Lisa Saddler is a pseudonym. With the exception of public personalities, all names and certain identifying factors are altered to preserve confidentiality.

Some previously recorded material has been edited for clarification.

Introduction

When our older son "Marc" was 11, he once said to me, "You know Mom, sometimes I'm so glad I'm growing up and will become a man. Then, there are other times when I want to stay a little boy." This book is for those who have found that life is a succession of leaving childhood behind, and embracing the adult responsibility and rapture of discovering a vision of themselves.

In my trek to comprehend the essence of not only my own clairvoyance but universal consciousness, I've spent a lifetime researching parapsychology, world religions, metaphysics and prophetic dreams. I've led workshops, prayer and meditation groups, participated in retreats, and counseled as a spiritual adviser. The first to write about parapsychology in a United States major newspaper, my weekly column "ESP & You" was carried by the *Akron Beacon Journal* in 1969-70 when we lived in the area. I'm a retired hatha yoga teacher dedicated to a healthy and active physical lifestyle, an environmentalist and a world traveler.

Precognitive dreams and psychic journeys have been an integral part of my spiritual vitality. Yet, my awe of an all-encompassing timeless, spaceless consciousness never ceases.

Introduction

I've danced to prescient symphonies without instruments, seen the glow of visions in the darkness. I've explored for mysteries shackled in rocks and fjords and glaciers, and listened to the thunder of waves and the hush of mountains. I've pondered at wise men and dedicated scientists and marveled at the magic of newborn babies. And over and over again I've validated that each soul, in its odyssey as an individualized child of a unifying cosmos, has access to knowledge beyond currently understood scientific laws, unfolding at the pace of the seekers evolutionary reach.

So as you turn the pages of this book culled from decades of my journals, you will discover many aspects of your own quest for a balance of intellect, wisdom, and spiritual dimension.

Most of all, you will cherish and nurture the mosaic rhythm of life in all its seasons.

L. S.

THE SOUL'S PROGRESS

A Time for All Seasons

Chapter 1

The Cosmos' Call

The wake-up flow of music from our clock radio was a welcome intrusion as I struggled to break away from my dream. To return to terrestrial terrain, I had one of two escapes: acknowledge the unacceptable and review the message to allow its imprint on my psyche; or, reject its relevance and deliberately block recall.

Like saying "No thank you," to an overture, I rejected the dream. Life was once again ambling into its comfort zone, and I wasn't going to allow even a sliver of a cloudburst to storm our calm. Scooting up in bed, I leaned against my pillows and let the waves of melody soothe my scrambled soul. Ordinarily, Jake bounced out of bed before the sun lit the skies. This morning, he was still asleep. I knew he'd been putting in long hours, and deserved a rest.

The cool fragrance of our wedding anniversary roses bobbed everywhere. Traipsing to the kitchen, I thought, Can't believe we've been married thirty years. Thirty years and two days to be exact. God, we were so young—just 21 and 22.

The first time Jake formally came to see me (with chaperon present, of course), his sea-blue eyes baiting mine, he extended a posy of baby-pink miniature rosebuds. My heart had raced like a gazelle in flight. Even out of his snappy U. S. Army uniform, this Paul Newman look-alike exuded all that I wanted. Later, with the United States embroiled in the Korean War, my brother Richard had challenged my non-conforming tenacity to wed an alien from our culture. "Okay," he pointed out, "you're going to go to the other side of the world with this guy. What will you do if he's killed in the war, leaving you with children to raise all by yourself in a foreign land?"

"If he should get killed in the war, we would at least have had time together," I explained. "And if I do have children to raise alone, I'll have a part of him with me."

Now, continents away from where it had all began, while the coffee perked, I drew the living-room draperies aside and, standing at our French doors, marveled at the flame of royal-purple bougainvillea hugging the building across the lawn.

This promised to be a dynamic summer day. I was scheduled for an early evening interview, for executive assistant to a prestigious corporation president. With the State Contractors' License exam behind him, Jake was becoming more and more optimistic about his new career direction.

I entered the bedroom chirping, "Sleepy head, I've brought you coffee. Are you awake?" He didn't appear to hear me. I got closer. "Sweetheart, coffee's ready." For just a micro-second, the sorcery of the dream slithered into my consciousness. Then Jake murmured something. Aha! It was going to be all right. "Would you rather sleep, or get up?"

"No, I'll get up," he said, easing against the headboard. He sounded hoarse, and a little groggy.

I handed him his cup. "Are you getting a cold?"

"Naa, not me," he sniffed.

Jake had always bragged about how very seldom he got sick, and even if he were getting a cold I knew he'd rebound fast. As we went through our workday morning routine, now and then a foreboding flare tinged my spine, but determined to deflect any negativity I'd snub the intruder.

When I was ready to leave, Jake was in the shower. "I'm going now," I hollered from inside the bedroom door. "Don't forget, I have that interview after work, so I'll be late."

"Lisa, wait a minute," he shouted back.

Chapter 1

I stopped. "Okaayy!" Placing my briefcase on the dresser, I thumbed through its contents. Résumé, references, street map—everything in its right place.

I heard the shower curtains slide. "Is this the day?"

"Yesss,"

"How late are you going to be?"

"I don't know. The appointment's at five," I said, running my hand down the sharp pleats of my white linen skirt. "I'm going in early and taking a short lunch break. Probably not too late though. Maybe six-thirty or so."

"Well," Jake said, above the volley of the waters. I was going to walk back into the bathroom to hear him better but he added, "Okay. It's nothing," and drew the curtains.

"I'll call you later. I'll see you tonight," I sang as I left, my navy blue linen blazer draped over an arm.

Isolated in my car, that ominous dream nudged for recognition. I turned up the radio, and deliberately focused on the bursts of pinks and yellows landscaped along the throughway. And of course Lilies of the Nile. Those explosions of lilac petals surging skyward on sturdy stems, so far-removed from their namesake, that grande dame whose banks were my coming-of-age playground.

Jake was now happy establishing his own business. It had to feel good, being productive again. Wasn't going to be all fun and games at 52, but there's a different type of satisfaction in working for oneself. He'd been in high spirits the last few weeks, putting together a construction proposal for a building in a nearby Air Force base, and even though his wasn't the winning bid, there was a new spring to his step. He'd joined a flying club, he'd resumed playing racquetball and was talking about joining the nearby Athletic Club. He'd even stopped smoking for a while. And I knew he could do it again—for good.

The morning flew. At my lunch break, I practiced yoga for a short interlude, then while having a sandwich at my desk chatted by phone with Shirley, a close friend. At a minute past one I noted, "Got to get to work now," and had barely placed the receiver down when the phone rang as if someone had been parked on the line, waiting.

"Hi, this is Lisa," I said thinking it was an internal call.

A woman's guarded voice asked, "May I please speak to Lisa Saddler."

"This is Lisa Saddler."

The caller identified herself as Carol Thompson, a nurse in the Emergency Room of Kaiser Hospital.

"Yes?" I wondered whether she was trying to get in touch with someone in our division and couldn't reach the department secretary.

She hesitated, then in a low, pacifying tone announced, "Mrs. Saddler, your husband, Jake, had a——a problem. And they brought him here."

A problem? Jake? What kind of a problem? My heart began to thump. Had there been a car accident? Was he flying? Was there an air crash? Who brought him there? I opened my mouth, but no words came out. I couldn't breathe.

"We thought you'd want to be here," the nurse said.

I sprang to my feet rolling my chair away. "How's he doing?" I said. All I wanted to know was how he was. Again she hesitated. Had she heard me? My heart hammered at my ribs. My knees were wobbling. I pulled my chair back and flopped down grasping the receiver with both hands, pressing it hard to my ear. I wanted to say more, but the membranes in my throat had crowded together, choking my vocal cords.

Still in her smooth, soothing manner the nurse said, "They're working on him now."

That was good. She seemed so much in control and at ease, everything had to be okay. But, how would I find them? "Do I just come to Emergency?" I managed.

Chapter 1

"Yes," Carol said. "Yes. When you get here, tell the receptionist who you are."

"I'll be there," I heard myself say. "Thank you."

My head buzzed as if a private plane had just penetrated my skull. Placing my palms on the desk, I tried to take a deep breath. I had to stay in control. I'm not alone, I repeated to myself.

I wasn't alone because, only nine months earlier, we'd moved thousands of miles to relocate near family. Strictly guided by a cosmic alert.

I picked up the phone.

For as far back as I remember, I've sought answers to Why, Where, When. Born into an Armenian Christian nuclear family in a village a stone's throw from Khartoum, the capital of Sudan, we transferred into the big city when I was 4. I grew up in Sudan, Africa's largest country, surrounded by multi-ethnic communities with divergent religious doctrines: Islamic, Jewish, Christian, Buddhist, Hindu, Atheist, Naturalist, Pagan. One of my closest friends was a fastidious Indian Hindu. Another, meticulously practiced Orthodox Judaism. A high-school classmate, the first black female to attend a higher education school in the country, was steeped in pagan rituals. Around me there were people of numerous dogma, each convinced that theirs alone was the only truth. This made me perceive early on, that although people were often contradictory and divisive in their religious beliefs, the unexplained phenomena of prophetic dreams, clairvoyance and altered states of consciousness was universal.

And as I grew older, it became increasingly apparent to me that I experienced more of these prodigious phenomena than anyone I knew.

Starting kindergarten before my 4th birthday, I graduated from an all-girls Church of England high school at 14, the youngest in their history. I was offered a full college medical scholarship to Cambridge, in an education program co-sponsored by Great Britain and the government of Sudan. It was 1944. With World War II raging in Europe, my widowed mother (who worked as the principal of the local Armenian Elementary School at a time when women remarried for security and stayed home), refused to dispatch a daughter into the war zone.

Comboni College for Boys, the only school of advanced education in town, run by Roman Catholic priests, allowed our Protestant high school principal, Miss Chandler, to teach college courses to girls after the boys left in the evening. There were no other options; I got a job as a typist clerk in a British import/export company, and enrolled in Miss Chandler's college classes.

At 16 I had advanced to working for the British government as a private secretary. Following a summer vacation in the mountains by the Red Sea, I caught a cold which developed into life-threatening pneumonia, necessitating the miracle antibiotic, penicillin, to be flown in from England specifically for my therapy. After a two-month hospital stay, I was convalescing at home, when I contracted progressive double pleurisy. My prognosis was grim.

On the morning I was to be transferred to the hospital, as dawn was breaking something gently prodded me. Sensing a dazzling radiance, I thought I was dreaming. After blinking several times, I closed my eyes. Some sort of communication, not really a voice, instructed "This is not a dream. This is real."

Cautiously, I opened my eyes. There was a luminous white figure immersed in a large oval-shaped incandescent bluish light hovering just above the side of my bed. I wasn't afraid. It was just there, like a big silver balloon. And for some reason, I wasn't surprised. Calmly, not knowing why, I simply watched as if waiting for instructions. The tranquil entity in that glow lifted an arm (the right one), and pointing straight at me, in a

Chapter 1

clear, precise cadence as if it were a benediction, pronounced, "You are now completely healed." After a brief wait for the words to sink in, the star-like brilliance and the form simply disappeared.

Gradually, familiar sounds and aromas of a spreading sunrise replaced the suspended animation, restoring my world to its comfortable normalcy. Was I supposed to go back to sleep? As I'd often done, I experimented with my breathing. It was still wheezy, short and labored, but, with each additional try I was now able to take longer and longer breaths. And my lungs hurt less and less.

In Sudan, we all slept outdoors. I climbed out of bed, eased into my slippers and trying to make as little noise on the cement veranda as I could, tottered inside. On an upright armchair in the living room, in my cotton pajamas sprinkled with gold and yellow daisies, I tucked my legs under me and waited for the others.

Mother came in first. On seeing me she froze, grabbed a quilt from the couch and rushed to my side crying, "Oh, my sweety, what are you doing? You know you shouldn't be out of bed."

"Mother, you're not going to believe this, but I don't have to go to the hospital. I'm well." I asserted.

"Of course you're well" she hastened, stretching the quilt to my shoulders shoving the edges around my body. "You're going to get completely well, and before you know it you'll be home again."

Composed, as if it were an every-day happening, I said, "Mother, you don't understand. I'm healed. Jesus told me this morning that I'm healed."

"Jesus?"

"Yes. He was in a light."

"A light? What light?"

"Oh, a beautiful brilliant light. It was so white."

Mother leaned close. "When?" I gazed at her terrified big, glistening ebony eyes on her oval face framed in mounds of long, silky black hair which knotted on top. "Lisa tell me, when was this?"

"It was this morning, Mom. Everyone was still asleep."

Pushing away wisps of hair clinging to the sides of her temples, Mother scrutinized my face closely. "This morning? Are you all right?" She pressed her ice-cold palm on my forehead. "Are you running a temperature?" she said as if speaking to herself, while her fingers glided down to my cheek. "No, you don't feel like you have a fever." She lifted my chin. "Let me see your eyes, Sweety. Stick your tongue out. Let me see your tongue."

Mother's whole world were her four children. How could I make her understand that she wasn't going to lose me? "Mom, I don't have to go. Really, I don't."

Mother kept shaking her head, wringing her hands, pacing around my chair. In her cotton robe, I watched her slender body shudder, her knees vibrate. "Yes, yes, my sweet child. Yes," she repeated. "I understand what you're saying."

But I knew she didn't believe me.

Still in my pajamas, still wrapped in grandma's soft, green and white and blue checkered quilt, my older brother Gregory, his features somber, his arms stiff, carried me out to the car where Richard sat at the wheel with the engine running. My 12-year-old sister Mary, Mother and I huddled together in the rear seat. Gripping my hands, her voice barely audible, Mother prayed, "Holy Virgin Mary. You're a mother too. You understand. I beseech you, please, please don't take my daughter away from me."

At our arrival, looking somber, four doctors went into action. The day was a blur of X-rays and needles and tests, flapping white coats and soft-spoken capped nurses. Late the next evening, as my brothers paced the floor and Mary and Mother sat on my bed, an orderly approached the men. The head physician wanted to speak to them, he said. Mother's lips moved in a silent rhythm.

Eventually, Greg and Richard came back accompanied by two nurses and a wheelchair. "You don't need to stay," Greg announced. "We're going home." The X-rays had shown a complete disappearance of what had previously been diagnosed as an advanced inflammation of the pleura. At the beginning of the following month, I was well enough to resume sprinting to my office on my bike, and volleying tennis tournaments with my team.

When I was 18, our family moved to Eritrea, a former Italian colony in breathtaking mountainous terrain neighboring Ethiopia, just a short hop by air from where in 1974 Donald Johanson discovered the 3.2 million-year partial skeleton of "Lucy." We settled in Asmara, Eritrea's capital nestled 8,000 feet above the Red Sea, and I started working as the private secretary to the British Commissioner of the Eritrea Police & Prisons. When the United States opened a Consulate in Asmara I was hired as Secretary to the Vice Consul, the only local female on their office staff.

Jake and I met in Greg's gift store in Asmara. I was 19, being courted by Tony, a resident physician whose old-money Italian family was one of the most prominent in town. Jake was 20, a staff sergeant in the United States Army Security Agency. We fell in love.

Point Four was creating special advanced college educational programs for third world countries, and the American Consul proposed that I become a candidate from Eritrea. Like the British medical scholarship in Sudan, this also required that graduates work in their country of origin for at least a two-year period. It would have meant a long separation for Jake and me. I opted not to apply.

To accommodate my family, we waited two years to get married, and immediately left Africa for the United States where he was reassigned to Alaska, and I eventually joined him. The Korean War ended, and after Jake's discharge, he started college in his home state of Indiana where Marc and Allen were born twenty months apart. And we continued to live in the Midwest.

As the political unrest in Africa escalated, my family trekked to the United States, settling in the San Francisco area. In keeping with cultural tradition, Mother and Mary made their home with Greg, who was single. Richard, with wife Valerie and two children, lived nearby.

It was 1977, four winters before nurse Carol Thompson's siren from ER. Jake and I had recently moved to Minnesota. California was in the middle of a flu epidemic. For over a year, my family had reeled on a roller-coaster of raised hopes and disillusioned valleys as Mary was carted in and out of hospitals with erratic debilitating-health symptoms, until, ultimately she was diagnosed with diabetes. Stabilized, as fragile as English bone china, Mary was steadily rallying when, during the Christmas holidays, she became ill with what her physician thought was just an intestinal bug. As January rolled around, Mary's condition deteriorated rapidly, and in the dark hours of late night she was transported by ambulance for exploratory surgery, which disclosed not the intestinal flu but acute peritonitis.

In less than ten days, Greg called to tell me that her vital signs had abruptly taken a dive, and suspecting a secondary infection she was being prepped for another invasive procedure.

That evening, I had just locked my desk for the weekend and was pulling up my boots to leave, when my boss came over. "Would you like to call from here to see how your sister's doing?" he suggested.

"Should I?"

"Sure, it'll save you a call," he offered.

Chapter 1

I located Greg at his accounting services office. "Just came here to get some papers," he said. "I'm on my way back. They tell us she's stable. But, . . . It doesn't look good," he stammered. "They're not even sure if they were able to remove all of the infected areas."

I wanted to know all the details, but in typical Eastern European fashion, Greg, the over-protective provider, had always avoided discussing bad news with female members of the family. Now he sounded so vulnerable. "It's going to be all right Greg," I lied, wishing I could put my arms around him. "I'll come out."

"Be prepared. And," he added in that low monotone, "be brave, dear sister." I hated to hear that phrase "Be brave." It always meant something bad that I needed to be brave about. And many times, I didn't want to be brave.

Outside my office, gobs of silver flakes twinkled in the parking lot lights, and the deep, powdery snow crunched under my boots as I stumbled to my car. Mechanically, I scraped and scrunched and brushed the snow off of the windows, then scooted into the driver's seat plunged my head down on the steering wheel and sobbed. Before I had even started the engine, my car was once again blanketed in white like an igloo. With my windshield wipers on full speed barely clearing space for me to see through, my headlights reflecting only a bluish tunnel in the whistling blizzard, I hobbled the slippery twelve miles home.

Inside, I threw my briefcase on the living room floor and fell weeping into an armchair. Jake came in from the kitchen. "What's wrong Lisa?" he said, flipping on the lights and kneeling by my chair. "Are you all right?" I nodded. Reaching over, he cupped my face in his hands. "Is it Mary?"

"She's very sick Jake," I whimpered.

Taking a folded handkerchief from his pocket, tenderly he dabbed my tears. "I'm so sorry, Sweetheart," he murmured.

"I've got to go there."

Clasping my hands as if they were fine bone china, he hugged them to his chest. "What can I do to help you?"

Those sensual, caring eyes bore through to the essence of my ordeal. "Can you get me on an early morning flight to San Francisco?"

"I'll call right away," he said, caressing my fingers. "Lisa, did you drive in this blizzard?" I nodded. "You should've called me. Or left your car at work and called a cab, Sweetheart." This was our first winter in Northern Minnesota and I was still learning to handle my car on sheets of ice. Wrapping his arms around my knees, he said, "Lisa, listen to me. A long time ago—even before I'd met you—I learned that things turn out for the best, whether we understand it or not. Mary's been suffering for so long."

"Why can't she get better?" I wailed. "Why does she have to go through so much? Of all people, why the one person who's never had a bad thought in her life? Never done anyone any wrong. Why?"

Standing, he pulled me close, cradling and rocking me like a newborn baby. "It's okay. It's okay," he whispered. "Shsh. I'll call the airlines. And after you eat something, I'll make you a hot toddy. It'll help you sleep."

The next morning, I was on a ten-thirty flight to be with a family waiting for the arrival of a daughter, who in the past had always generated hope by her unfaltering trust in the goodness of a personal, loving Father.

In San Francisco, after a rushed dinner, Greg, Richard, Valerie and I, drove in a furious rainstorm to the ICU where we were quickly checked through. But nothing had prepared me for that surreal theatre. Mary's comatose, draped, bloated body lay on a white-sheeted high structure, imprisoned by wires hooked to

Chapter 1

blinking and beeping electronics, with screens that pulsed with lines of black and green and red.

As I stood by her, through that bond my sister and I had shared all our lives, I clearly heard her silent plea, "See what they're doing to me?"

I didn't recognize that swollen face with hair matted down, eyes taped shut, a long, curved tube coming out of her open mouth. I couldn't watch that heaving machine forcing the rhythm of life into her weary lungs like a relentless bulldozer. My stomach churned. My head reeled.

Speechless, I slipped out and on shaky legs stood by her door. Valerie followed me, and side by side, shoulders touching, hands clasped, we listened to Greg's despondent calls, "Maaree, Maaree, Maaree. Wake up!"

"The doctors have told us to talk to her," Val explained.

"I know."

"He's a basket case. I've never seen him like this."

"I know."

"You think she hears him? Knows we're here?"

I nodded.

Later, the brothers came out. We rode the elevator down, scrambled into our car and with the smash of the wind and the crash of waters at our windshield mirroring our dejection, drove the twenty miles home in utter silence.

The next evening, we had planned to return to that chamber that wrenched my core. After dinner, while Mother was preoccupied with loading the dishwasher, I scampered over to the others who were putting on their coats in the hallway and whispered, "I'm not going with you guys tonight."

Valerie gave me a quizzical look. "You aren't?"

Motioning them away from the kitchen door I gulped, "No, I'm not. I want to remember my sister the way she really was. Not what she's been transformed into with all that paraphernalia." In a louder tone I said, "I'm going to stay with Mother tonight. You go ahead."

Not looking directly at each other, saying only what needed to be said, Mother and I completed our cleanup. As we started for the living room, I suggested, "Would you like me to read anything from the Bible to you, Mom."

"No, thank you." She stopped. Her twitching fingers clutched my arm. Slowly, she spun around. Her face was the color of ashes in the fireplace. "A parent loves all of her children. As a mother, you know that," her voice quivered. "And you know that I love my Val and Jake like I do my own. But somehow, a mother becomes closer to the person who needs her most."

After the others returned, Valerie and I sneaked away. "Mary's just not there," she sighed. "It's excruciating, seeing her like that."

Barely twenty hours later, before rushing away again, the family had regrouped in the living room for after-dinner coffee. Curled like a kitten under the blue afghan I had knitted for her, my tranquilized mother slept in her favorite armchair. Greg was slouched in the corner of the sofa with his legs stretched out under the glass coffee table, his stoic chestnut eyes staring at the floor. On the love-seat, their fingers intertwined, Richard and Val leaned against each other. I sat on a straight armchair, feet firmly planted at the edge of the maroon and brown Oriental carpet. Mom's much loved sugar-almond cookies lay untouched on a white porcelain platter.

The moment had come for me to prepare the family.

"Remember when I was here in August for Mary's birthday?" I said. "Mary told me about an experience, which she hadn't told anyone."

Greg lifted his cup and took a sip of coffee. Richard and Valerie looked to me. "I'm not surprised," Val said.

"If you remember, the last time Mary was hospitalized, her heart stopped once. Completely. It was the time doctors said

Chapter 1

she'd gone into a diabetic coma. And she had to be resuscitated."

"I remember that," Richard said turning to his wife, "Don't you?"

"Of course I do," Val nodded.

"Mary told me, during that incident she'd found herself in a beautiful garden. She said, 'You know Lisa, the wonderful part was, I had no pain. Here I was in the most enchanting place you've ever seen. I felt so alive, so free, so airy just like a breeze. And no pain. It was wonderful.' You should have seen her face. She was absolutely glowing."

"She didn't say anything to us," Val offered. I heard a sigh from Greg.

"She said a nurse later told her, 'Mary, you really scared us.' And you know what else?" I curled my twitching feet tightly around each other pulling them close. "Mary told me she hadn't wanted to come back—that there were times she wished she hadn't."

Silence, like a sheathing shroud, cloaked our taut circle. Then Valerie challenged, "Did Mary really say that? Did she?"

I struggled to keep my voice steady. "Yes. She did." Richard's eyes narrowed. He glanced at Mother's sleeping form, hesitantly examined each of us.

"We all know . . . We all know that Mary's hanging on for our sakes. She's been suffering so much. It's brutal." Greg's head hunched and he shifted his weight as if a barbell had just settled on his shoulders. "We have to let her go," I said. "We're going to have to let her return to her Creator—for *her* sake."

I telegraphed a silent message to Mary, Okay dear Sister, I've done my part—I know it's what you want. All of us sat there, eerily immobile. Outside, the wind whined through the palm branches. The rain continued to pummel the picture windows.

Richard stood, strolled to the window, then lumbered to the edge of our circle. With his hands in his pockets, he pivoted to Greg. "What do you say? We won't go tonight?"

Throwing his head back, Greg closed his eyes. And we waited. It was as if every formerly animate object in that room had receded into a paralyzed standstill. After what seemed like forever, wearily dragging his legs in as the heels of his shoes scraped grooves like railroad tracks on the carpet, Greg turned to me. His face was a chiseled mask of acceptance. In the soft lights, his eyes glistened with moisture. "All right," he acquiesced. It was barely a whisper.

All the lights blinked off, then came on again. A crack of thunder woke Mother, who, jumping to her feet demanded, "What's happening?"

"It's okay, Mother, we're all here," Greg was in control again. "But Richard and Val are going home now."

After they left I strode with Mother to her room where, reaching down, I gathering her tiny, quavering frame in my arms. "Good night Mom, I'll see you in the morning," I said. "It's after ten. Sleep well."

With trembling lips Mother kissed me on each cheek, and shuffled past her bed to the dresser. She removed her glasses and cautiously placing them next to a profusion of family pictures, swiveled around and for a few seconds just stared at me with blank eyes. Then, raising her unsteady arms to the heavens implored, "May God have mercy on us." This God of my mother, whom she had always credited with helping raise her orphaned children, was now threatening to abandon her.

What could one say? Facing the loss of an offspring had to be the cruelest fate of a parent. I stepped out and shut her door behind me as a hint of Jean Nate' wafted out from Mary's bathroom.

With hail rat-a-tatting on the roof, the winds howling at my window, I crawled into bed and stretched the covers to my quivering chin. It had been a grueling three days. And the

Chapter 1

weather had matched our passions. In bed, I thought maybe now that we've surrendered, this good, personal God of ours, through some miraculous healing, will give back my sister.

I slid into my nightly meditation ritual. Starting with the end of the day and continuing backward to the beginning, I focused on positive events for which I could be thankful. The fury of the storms had taken its toll in the Bay Area, but I was grateful that Greg's house was standing firm. I was thankful for Mother's health. Mother, our inspiration and role model, who, no matter how lacking we were in material possessions, always reminded us, "Look at others worse off." I was thankful for the strength to ask the family for Mary's release, and especially grateful for their reaction. I was so thankful for the love that nurtured us: Greg at 55, the gallant protector; 52-year-old Richard who brought Valerie into the family just after I'd flown away with a new husband.

I was thankful for the tranquil, healing influence of my Jake, always my hero, whose daily phone calls reminded me of one of the reasons I had fallen in love with this man. I was thankful for the support and concern of our wonderfully balanced sons Marc and Allen.

And, I was thankful for the joys and laughter that Mary and I had shared, especially at exhilarating spiritual retreats.

Look at others who are worse off. I fell asleep to the echo of those words.

Suddenly, I was awakened by an insistent glow as if a full moon had ruptured layers of black clouds and was saturating every atom of my room. I lay absolutely still, careful not to disturb whatever it was bidding recognition. I listened. Outside, the turmoil and thunder and lightning had completely vanished. Inside, the house was suspended in a rhythmic hush.

Without having to look at the clock, I knew that it was just after one. I also remembered that I was in my mother's home. Slowly, I opened my eyes and transfixed, acknowledged a phosphorescent magnetism that had eclipsed everything. In the hush of the cosmic cadence, I recalled the hypnotic radiance that had awakened me three decades earlier in that far away land of the Nile, forever frozen in the secrets of my soul. I looked for another person. There was no one. I listened for voices. Nothing.

Seamlessly, the brilliance dissolved into the darkness but the hum of the cosmos pounded my consciousness.

Of course, Mary's had a divine healing, I reasoned. We released her. We let her go, and now God has restored her to us where she belongs. And she will be home again. And our mother will be happy again. And all will be well with our world.

I dared not move. I dared not make a sound. Something was happening. I knew something was happening. And it was going to be good.

A dog started to bark. Then stopped.

As I lay motionless inhaling the silence that saturated the dark, a screeching knell whipped through the hush, spurting my body into the air. My heart throbbed.

I heard Greg say, "Hello."

Shoving the bedcovers off, I grabbed my robe and wrapping it tight around my body, tiptoed to his partially open door.

Chapter 2

The Sun Also Sets

Outside Greg's bedroom, I listened. "Yes, yes—yes," he was saying. Then, I heard the bolt of his dull murmur, "She died, huh?"

I slid the door open. Greg was sitting up in bed, bathed in the emerald sheen of his clock radio. Stepping in, I closed the door gently until I heard the click of the latch, and as if propelled by a gust at my back went and stood by his bed.

The numbers on the clock changed to 1:35 with the red pointer indicating A.M. "Okay," he whispered into the phone, "that's all right," and as he leaned over to put the receiver back, grasping it from his hand I placed it on the stand, then switched the bedside lamp on. Greg covered his head with both hands, and began to shake with dry sobs.

I eased down on the bed. "She's finally resting," I said hugging him. "She's at peace."

Tearless, like a wind-up toy that someone else had started, I rocked him.

Was this real? Could Greg be mistaken? Like comforting a child awakened from a nightmare, I rocked him, and rocked him. Apparently, they hadn't asked that someone go to the hospital. Why not? When his sobs lessened, I heard my alien voice, "It's still very early in the morning, Greg. Why don't you try to get some sleep?"

In the hallway, I noted that Mother's door was undisturbed, her room silent. She hadn't heard a thing. And like a robot, tearless, I tramped back to my bedroom.

Because she was so easy to get along with, Mary and I had shared the gold-mines of sisterhood. And, especially in recent years, had appreciated attending spiritual retreats where together we laughed and cried, and sang and sat in silence, and climbed hills and stumbled in valleys in re-discovering the synergy of renewal. Even when Mary and I were physically apart, our telepathic bond aligned us. I understood her shyness, her insecurities. She forgave my overbearing need to teach my "little sister" the tools of my discoveries.

Until that night, I had not been traumatized by the loss of an intimate family member, for my dad had died soon after Mary's birth when I was only a child. In my early teens, the only grandmother I knew (my paternal), died after a long bout with tuberculosis. That had illustrated the orderly laws of the universe: Grandma was old, and after being sick for a long time, Grandma died. That was the nature of life. As an adult, the closest I'd come to a death in the family was when Sport, our Labrador retriever, had succumbed to old age. Even then, Jake had thwarted my personal involvement with the process of expiration, as he alone kept vigil by Sport's side.

Now, some stranger had said that my only sister died. Couldn't be. They had to be wrong! She was the youngest in our family, how could she die? And what was death anyway? And, why was it that so many years ago I had been instantly healed, and now, alerted by an identical cosmic glow, Mary was gone.

And most importantly, I had expected that somehow my sister would say good-bye to me. She didn't.

I thought of a time, years ago, when we lived in the Chicago area. Pauline, a manic depressive most of her adult years, was a student in a spiritual study group I led. One morning, in that twilight state between sleep and wakefulness, I saw Pauline breeze into my bedroom demanding my attention. "Okay, I'm up," I yielded, "what are you doing in my bedroom?"

Chapter 2

With a cock-sure, devil-may-care toss of her head Pauline announced, "I did it. I went and did it."

"What did you do?"

"I put an end to the whole thing."

"Pauline, what whole thing?"

Flitting around like a featherweight ballerina she warbled, "This is it. I'm on my way. I'm leaving." And very pleased with herself, faded away in a pirouette. I knew, in a cosmic reach, Pauline had just informed me that she'd done something to end her life.

I waited till our boys left for school, then discussed the incident with Jake, adding, "I don't know what to do. She seemed so determined. Should I be calling her husband?"

"It sounds as if she's already done it," he suggested. "But if it'll make you feel better, call." I tried and tried; couldn't get through. And since I was scheduled to participate in an all-day spiritual seminar, left. On my return, Marc, then 7, met me at the door to say Pauline's sister wanted me to know there had been an accident and she was in the hospital.

When I reached her, Pat cried, "Pauline attempted suicide. We've been trying to get you all day."

"I'm so sorry, Pat. How?"

"Sleeping pills. They don't know how much. It's touch-and-go. She didn't get up at her usual time this morning, and when Walt tried to wake her up he couldn't."

I rushed to the hospital emergency ward. "Oh, Lisa" Walt, her husband, sobbed, "she's almost gone."

A middle-aged physician hugging a chart ambled over. "She'll probably not make it," he said. "You should be with her now if you want to." Then turned to me, "Are you her daughter?"

"No, just a very close friend."

Sixty-four-year-old Pauline recovered.

Now my sister, two decades younger, was pronounced dead. I thought we had an unspoken agreement that she would at least say to me, "I'm leaving." Or was the light her pure entity in transition?

The sun had not cracked the dawn, when Greg phoned Richard and bolted for the hospital while Mother still slept. A couple of hours later, the doorbell rang. Preoccupied with tying the sash of her robe, Mother came out of her room heading toward the door. How does one tell a Mother that her youngest, her reason for living, is gone?

I blocked her way. "Mom, I'll get it, I'm dressed." She looked up at me as if halted in a sleepwalk. "Breakfast is all ready," I said, putting an arm around her shoulders to direct her toward the kitchen.

Her melancholy eyes searched mine. "Where's Greg?"

The doorbell rang again. Without answering her, I began walking away, and Mother padded behind me. At the front door, Richard stood with an arm propped against the wall, his face a somber mask, gazing down at the welcome mat. He glanced at Mother, then gave me a quizzical look. "Good morning," I emphasized, shaking my head No.

"'Morning. Did you sleep well, Mom?" he said, stepping in.

As I reached over to close the door, Mother pushed it open and shuffled out on the landing still wet from the rains, her gaze sweeping the road. "Where's Val?" she asked.

"Come on in Mom. Val's following me," Richard said, tenderly holding her close, leading her to the couch.

On the soft pillows, Mother sat up rod-straight like a lioness who's been alerted that one of her cubs is going to be snatched away. "Val's following you?" she gulped, shifting closer to scrutinize his demeanor. "What are you doing here so early?" Then, swirling around to me challenged, "Why are they coming? What's going on? Why isn't Greg here?"

I turned away from her terror.

Chapter 2

Vaulting up, Mother spun me around, piercing my shield with her prying glare. "Oh my God," she shrieked, "my Mary's gone, isn't she? Isn't she?" and swinging around to Richard screamed, "No, no, no!" as he carried her limp body back to the couch. And together they wept. "Oh, my dearest, dearest God," Mother wailed, "where are you? Where are you? I knew. I knew last night she was gone. How am I going to live without my Mary?"

When Valerie arrived, we gave Mother a tranquilizer, then in the kitchen wrapped ourselves around each other. I could finally allow myself to begin mourning.

Greg called just after Richard and Valerie left. "You should see how peaceful Mary looks." His voice was calm, almost buoyant. "There's a smile on her face, and such a glow, you wouldn't believe it."

"Really?"

"Really. Everybody's saying so."

"Greg, stay in the hospital. Rich and Val are on their way."

"Did you tell them?"

"No."

"Did they call the hospital?"

"I don't know Greg. I thought you must have told them this morning. Didn't you?"

"I just said come as soon as you can. I didn't tell them why," Greg said. "I'll go and watch for them."

In her tranquilized sleep, Mother didn't hear Valerie return alone from the hospital, so we sneaked into my bedroom. "Of course we knew why Greg was calling that early in the morning," Val shrugged. "As soon as the phone rang, we knew. God, how our sweet Mary suffered. It's amazing! You wouldn't think it's the same person. She looks so serene. It's as if her beautiful spirit has taken wings like a butterfly and all that's left is her shell now. I don't know whether it's your influence, Lisa, but for the first time in my life I really believe that the physical body is just a temporary home for the real self. I don't think I've ever seen her look so peaceful, so beautiful. There's a glow about her and a smile at the corners of her lips."

We heard mother stirring and went over. "Oh my Val," she moaned, "where is she? Where's my daughter?"

Valerie sat by her side. "Mama, believe me she's with all of us now. She's finally out of her misery. She'll be with you so much more beautifully than ever before."

Pushing herself up on one arm, leaning close Mother sighed, "You're lying. You're lying to me."

"Mama, have I ever lied to you? Have I? Tell me just one time when I've lied to you. You're the one who's told me many, many times how after Baba died you felt his presence with you all the time, helping you raise the children. Remember? Didn't you tell me that?"

"Yes." Mother sank back on the pillows. "He was with me all the time. I knew he was helping me."

"Okay. Now Mary will be with you all the time, Mama."

The doorbell kept chiming, flowers arrived, friends came with food, and the phone shrilled incessantly.

In my sister's room, I pulled the draperies open to let the California sunshine sparkle through. I chose the best flower arrangement—flaming ruby roses nestled in white baby's breath on a platter of evergreens with white carnations—and placed it on the dresser, infusing Mary's personal space with the fragrant essence of life. I fluffed the embroidered toss pillows, smoothed out the pale pink bedspread, the way I had seen Mary do so many times.

Greg asked me to help him choose an outfit for the burial. He said that the funeral director had requested something with a high neckline. Being preoccupied with having to make mundane decisions is a good distraction from having to confront an immediate trauma, and yet, as I fingered through Mary's wardrobe, my heart ached with the reality of a sister's absence. I

Chapter 2

gazed at her closet reflecting the neat, orderly personality she was. Everything was color-coded and arranged symmetrically–winter clothes out, summer items put away in garment bags, shoes neatly side by side starting with dark conservative pumps and ending with low-healed loafers.

In the end, Greg wanted the white pants outfit with shiny gold decorator buttons I'd designed and tailored for Mary's size 7 figure. We added a sky-blue silk blouse with a bias scarf collar.

Greg suggested I accompany him to the funeral home. When we arrived, Mr. Neal, the director, gently examined the clothes we'd taken in individual plastic bags. He spread out the blouse and jacket with care on an armchair and turning around stretched the bag holding the pants out to me. "We won't need this," he smiled. "You may take it back."

What do you mean you won't need this, I frizzled. Of course you'll need it. I'm not going to have my sister lying there with no pants. I thrust the bag back into his hands. "No, no. We want her to wear the pants," I stressed.

Irene, his assistant, calmly took the bag. "Of course," she said softly. "We'll see that she wears the pants." And lovingly, as if it were a one-of-a-kind regal gown weighed down with priceless gems, draped it over her arm.

"Thank you." I offered a shaking envelope. "Here's the picture you asked for."

Tenderly, Irene removed the picture. "Oh" she exclaimed, leaning her head to one side, "she was so young."

Was? What's was? For a flash of a second, the past twenty-four hours hadn't happened. "She's only 44," I emphasized.

"So beautiful," Irene added. I knew she probably said that about everybody, but loved hearing it about my sister. "We'll do her hair exactly like this."

"Yes, thank you." Looking around, I liked what I saw. Although in the past I'd read that numerous options offered by the funeral industry were largely financially motivated, I realized that an aesthetic setting with a backdrop of soothing music, lush live plants and sensuous floral essences helped shroud the pain of sorrow. And I knew that Mary was somewhere in that building. I didn't want to step out into reality.

On the evening of the wake, her head held high while her body nestled under my arm quivered like a kitten rescued from a frozen pond, Mother walked into the funeral home between me and her 24-year-old granddaughter, Grace. At the end of the sanctuary, a high structure between tall multiple floral stands supported a shiny oak coffin with a huge spray of greenery and pink rosebuds cascading down the center. As we got closer I was startled to see Mary in her white jacket with the gleaming gold buttons and blue blouse holding a sprig of tiny violets, a white satin pillow cradling her head coifed exactly like the picture. Her eyes were closed. What was she doing, sleeping under that blanket of flowers while everyone buzzed around?

I sidled up close and put my hand on her long fingers—they were frigid. I cupped her glowing face—it was shockingly icy. They're right, I thought, there really is a brilliance. But aah, what do they know, she's just sleeping.

The doctors said Mary had died, but until my lips touched her frozen cheek, I had not understood that the active, physical body which had been a living, breathing segment of my world had somehow undergone an irreversible physical change. So, this is death, but exactly where is my sister?

In the private family area, I kept watching that body in the casket. Does she know that we're here? That her beloved mother is inconsolable? I kept watching for movements, for something to happen with which I was familiar. Nothing! This was the moment of reality—the absolute stillness of physical death.

The rituals began.

The choir's Gregorian chants, the priests' prayers, the congregation's joint voices pleading for forgiveness and mercy pulsated with the aroma of incense. If passion alone could have done it, heaven surely must have been shaken. At the end, everyone stood up and their voices bellowed the Lord's Prayer. Never had I welcomed a ritual more.

With a wan smile, his eyes brimming in empathetic sorrow, the family priest marched over to Mother. "Come on," he whispered holding out his hand, "let us go and say good-bye." Wait a minute dear God, this isn't the way it's supposed to be. This is against the laws of the universe. A person is born, gets old, then dies. Why are we saying good-bye to the youngest in our family?

I discovered why pageantry and rituals in traditional churches survive from generation to generation: the hypnotic drone of readings from the Scriptures; the choir's wails for mercy clashing with the exalted chants of praise; the shimmering gold and silver of vestments in cadence with icons and Bibles lifted to the skies in symbolic hope. All these re-focus our energies from individual self to a shared palette of universal consciousness where intoxicating highs and cataclysmic lows thrive side by side on this planet we call Earth.

I also discovered that after a loss, the mind often hesitates to acknowledge the irreversible finality of physical death and the formalities of wakes and funerals (or whatever form the living choose to gather together at times of loss) establish a focal reference point that does not accommodate denial.

In my journal, I wrote:

> I'm grateful that I was forced to participate in the activities from which I wanted to run away. I realize that those activities have been a psychological beginning point; a preparation for life without that person. When at times I find myself thinking of Mary in the old manner—I'll call Mary, I've got to tell Mary, Mary's got to know this—flashbacks of the wake and funeral shock me back into reality.

Leaving Mother knotted my stomach. Stoically she sat, enfolded in the arms of her granddaughter, her lips pinched together, her breathing in short spurts, as I slipped out.

Settled on the plane headed home, I closed my eyes, leaned back and concentrated on trying to re-gather my balance. So much had happened, so fast.

A time to be born, a time to die.

I remembered an encounter, five years earlier. Our closest friends Jeanne and Dennis were expecting their first child. Jeanne and I had met when she hired me to become editor of their cosmetic company newsmagazine and product brochure, and the instant chemistry between us spread into an extended family after she married Dennis. The four of us went on vacations together, even after Jake and I moved away.

Because Dennis had two sons from a previous marriage, this time they were hoping the new addition would be a daughter, and family, friends, office personnel, all predicted a baby girl.

Jeanne's pregnancy had gone into full-term when on a Saturday morning at pre-dawn I began to drift into the ethers of a cosmic panorama, and alerted my memory to etch its details. From the cusp of the horizon, a wave of misty blues and lavenders began approaching me and, as I concentrated, a form became distinct from the background. Bundled in the colors, a newborn baby, with a soft, rounded body all curled up drew nearer and nearer, until with slow deliberate rhythm, I reached out and the baby tumbled into my arms. Cradling it close to my body I looked into its sparkling deep blue eyes and recognized Jeanne and Dennis's unborn child on it's voyage of birth. A boy.

In the morning, I described my encounter to Jake. "No girl for Dennis either," he chuckled. "Are you going to tell them?"

When I phoned Jeanne, she said, "You sound excited."

Chapter 2

"I am. I met your baby."

"You did? I'm not surprised. I'm getting so big, and I'm so tired, and I hope you're going to say she's arriving soon."

"I don't know when, Jeanne. I do know it's a boy." There was utter silence. "Jeanne? Are you there?"

"Yes. Yes I am. Lisa, I think this time you're wrong. My mother's relatives in the South know these things, and they're all telling me it's a girl. I know you've been right so many other times. I'll never forget that time we were being sued and you dreamt of those white tablecloths. You told us everything would work out fine. It was such a relief. Remember?"

"Of course I do."

"And it worked out exactly as you said."

"Yes, that was a symbolic dream. This is different." I wanted to be sure that she understood. "This was a cosmic connection. I actually held your son in my arms. A perfect, healthy, chubby baby."

"We just want a healthy, normal baby," Jeanne said. "So, we'll have three boys. That'll be fine with us."

Four nights later, I heard Jake on the phone say, "Hey, congratulations," and grinning, handed me the receiver. "It's Dennis. Wants to talk to you."

"I don't know why I'm calling you," Dennis laughed. "Of course it's a boy. Kevin. You met him before we did."

Dreams. The elixir of songs and poetry. And visions—mostly unremembered or misunderstood.

When we lived in the area, I wrote a weekly column for the *Akron Beacon Journal* entitled "ESP & You." One of my readers asked me to interpret a dream she and her granddaughter had had at the same time, involving a cat and a mouse. To analyze this dream accurately, there was much I needed to know: First, had they possibly discussed cats and mice recently and under what circumstances. Second, did they like cats, and what do cats represent to them symbolically? If the dreamers had grown up in a British culture, the cats would have been interpreted as tidings of very good luck and prosperity. (It was only after I came to the United States that I found a black cat symbolizes *bad luck.*) Third, were they afraid of mice? Fourth, did they notice unusual colors? And foremost, was the dream experience such that they couldn't push it aside even when they were awake?

Although some symbols may have a more instant identification (like a wedding ring in cultures that use a ring to indicate marital status), in dreams, symbolism takes on a very personal identity. In most cultures water symbolizes a purification, a cleansing (as in baptism), but to those who do not swim, water may provoke a fear of impending danger. In addition, our psyches (our soul makeup) is such that a dream which may have a deep psychological meaning for one person may mean nothing, or something different, to another.

And, not all dreams are precognitive or carry a psychic statement. Many dreams can be just nonsense.

In the hypnotic drone of the engine on my flight back to Minneapolis after Mary's funeral, a song resonated in my head. *Sunrise, Sunset, . . . One season following another . . .*

It was only then that I allowed myself permission to acknowledge the death bulletin on the morning I left for San Francisco.

Just before dawn, like a far-away blinking star on a velvet night, an image had demanded my attention. No, no, no I'd insisted, go away. Rat-a-tat-tat, on and off, the icon signaled its urgency, until I acquiesced, All right, I'll concede, but I don't have to accept its relevance. And clearly, a pure white sheet, harshly bordered in raven black, began to flip in the zenith. A death announcement. In my ethnic background, there was no question that a death announcement was always framed in black. Because I'd been away from that culture for decades, it was easy to lull myself into dismissing the decree.

In an earlier journal I had written:

> Altered state messages appear to us in symbolism to allow the psyche to become acclimated to the communication—to choose not to accept if reality may be too painful at that moment. Especially, for those who are raised in a culture where symbolism is important and very much acceptable, it almost becomes the communication norm in dreams between our psyche and the cosmos.

When beginning in the mid 90s it became more acceptable to acknowledge interest in the message of dreams, *LIFE* Magazine's September 1995 cover story "New Science Reveals What Dreams Can Do For You," quoted Jungian therapist Robert Bosnak: "When you pay attention to your dreams, you begin to inhabit a much larger part of your soul."

Paying attention to dreams is my cultural heritage. To have been born and raised in Africa, accepted by most paleontologists as "the cradle of humanity," is my inheritance. Finding myself immersed in the ethers of the cosmos has been my destiny.

Chapter 3

On a Clear Day

The question of whether there really is a "life" after death has been mankind's most persistent mystery, and almost always considered subjectively dependent upon one's religious beliefs.

When in 1970, Dr. Elizabeth Kubler-Ross's book *On Death and Dying,* documented near-death experiences of persons with divergent religious beliefs, the term "out-of-body" became an accepted form of identifying near-death experiences. Publications of similar near-death experiences by Dr. Raymond Moody, Jr., beginning with *Life After Life,* in 1975 followed. These were true stories of real, ordinary people, some of whom had been pronounced clinically dead, thus introducing the acronym NDEs (Near Death Experiences).

Before the beginning of NDE books, an out-of-body experience was accepted in the world of psychic phenomena as the separation of the self consciousness (or the soul) from the physical body; and, very often, the observation of one's physical body from a point not occupying the same space.

In 1960, a decade before Kubler-Ross's precedent-setting publications, we lived in a suburb of Cincinnati, Ohio. My close friend, Nancy (the wife of our minister) and I, shared an insatiable thirst for understanding the soul beyond what was taught and accepted by the Christian churches. Breaking away from structured classes, we created our own study and prayer group comprised of other young mothers searching for meaningful spirituality. In our zeal to investigate all possible connections

Chapter 3

between mind, body and soul, we even utilized physical dance and movement techniques which, to appease the elders of the church, we dubbed Devotion In Motion.

That summer, a young, vivacious member of our congregation, Debbie, who also happened to be our Marc's kindergarten teacher, came down with a mysterious malady only four months after her wedding. Her family contacted our Group for prayers, and Nancy and I initiated a round-the-clock healing vigil.

Debbie had a miraculous recovery which astounded even her doctors. She was released from the hospital, and we celebrated our joy for answered prayers. Two weeks later, with no warning, Debbie died. She was 23.

Still in my 20s myself, I was not prepared for the shock of a promising, young vibrant person's death. Religious convictions which had previously supported my trust in a nurturing, fathering God made no sense any more. I abandoned my disciplined daily prayer, meditation and Bible study which had been an integral part of my life.

Less than a week after Debbie's death, after Jake had left for the office I was waiting for Marc and Allen, then 6 and 4, to wake up. It was early, around six-thirty. I went into our bedroom and lay down on the bed. This was my own personal time which, in the past, I'd used to study spiritual growth material. That morning, still shocked by Debbie's death I simply lay there listening to the chirping of the birds. A breeze bellowed the draperies at the open window back and forth carrying in whiffs of recently mowed grass, and a branch from our elm tree outside played a game of peek-a-boo swaying into view then disappearing.

The beginning of an ordinary Midwestern day.

I heard a whistling, like gentle sudden gusts whipping in the wind, which I thought was coming from outside. But as it grew in intensity I realized it was a pulsation in my ears, which transformed into high-pitched vibrations thoroughly absorbing the upper portion of my head and erasing all external noises. My eyelids started to drag, and I lost all sense of physical awareness. I thought I was falling asleep. Instead, I was locked into an altered state of consciousness that had numbed my body but sharpened my senses.

The vibrations accelerated into a musical cadence as if it were an approaching band, immersing me into its seismic orchestration. Wow, I thought, this must be what a celestial symphony sounds like!

I knew I was lying on my back, but didn't feel the hardness of the bed. I wanted to open my eyes—I couldn't. While my physical body felt lifeless, supported by the symphonic waves, I had the sensation of floating, completely unsaddled by gravity. It dawned on me that somehow I'd been lifted from my bed and was hovering in space like a silent, bladeless helicopter on "halt," with a clear vision of everything in the room. I glanced down at the bed expecting to see it empty and was jolted to find that my physical body was still lying there in my long, aster blue robe.

My first impression was, Oh God, I'm dying. I'm not ready to die. My second was, What will Marc and Allen do when they wake up and find their mother dead? I have to call their father and alert him to rush home, for the boys can't be left alone.

The phone was on the night stand on the left side of my bed; so as I had done many times before, I reached for the receiver. Nothing happened. The body on the bed refused to move because I wasn't in it. I tried to draw myself back into my physical body. I couldn't. What should I do next? I became very frightened.

My left arm is resting lightly on my body and all I have to do is lift it. My hand is partially closed, my wedding and engagement rings visible on my third finger. I concentrate every ounce of energy into moving that arm. It will not budge. Hoping that it's all a dream, I try to roll over—nothing happens. I continue to hover in the air and watch that body lie immobile as if it were a clay statue, everything about it absolutely lifeless. The real, live me, now existing in some sort of a mysterious dimension, has separated from my physical body, leaving it empty like a lonely, isolated shell washed ashore on the beach.

Much like doffing an outer layer of skin that at one time had been a protective element but is now no longer essential, I have shed my body. It is a very natural fruition; like a baby leaving behind a placenta that had previously sheltered and nurtured it. The separation is painless, effortless, and to my surprise, deeply fulfilling.

As I think of the birth of a baby, I recognize a thin, silvery substance sinuating from me to the motionless body on the bed. It appears to ribbon out from an area in the general direction of my chest, floating in an easy, rippling motion to my real self in a segregated somewhere. Without understanding how, I know that this is my lifeline to my physical body which I control. I know that as long as I do not sever this silver cord I will not die, and unafraid, I'm ready to continue whatever journey lies ahead.

With the celestial music supporting me, I allow myself to float away from my physical body. It is exhilarating. I feel totally alive and amazingly light with a purpose and self-identity I've never experienced before. Defying the laws of earth, gravity and physics, I pass through the bedroom ceiling as if it were simply composed of air, and find myself in a foreign environment—a theater created and sustained by our nurturing, maternal cosmos.

It is a place where there are many, many others, but no one appears to be aware of my presence. Without wanting to be obvious or in anyone's way, I simply watch. I don't know what my own body looks like, but I note that the others appear to be exquisitely fine, wispy energy forms: entities in a separate existence from the planet Earth, controlled by their thoughts and evolutionary self-identity consciousness.

This is the next level of the soul, I reason, the animating principle that evolves through its own self-awareness.

In the level of creative energy where I find myself, the ego-conscious (in our present expression clothed in a hard physical body) has acquired a soft, lightly-opaque form. I, too, must have taken on this type of composition allowing a freedom of movement unhindered by body weight or gravitational pull, fostering a deeper awareness of my own identity. It is a state of consciousness more real than life itself, and there is no question in my mind that the nucleus which had separated from my physical body is the real entity, the real soul, the real meaningful experience of existence. And I understand that physical death is each soul's natural, evolutionary progression.

The magnificent symphony of the spheres is everywhere. I love it, but am not ready to stay. My young children need me, and I have to go back.

With the thought that it is time to return to my home on the planet Earth, I feel the silver cord begin to shrink like an elastic band, now smoothly drawing me back. My return seems more accelerated than the journey away, and I find myself back in my bedroom where my physical body is waiting on the bed exactly the way I had left it. The silver substance contracts, and I slither into my body easily as if it were an overcoat that automatically opened and allowed me in, closing snugly over me.

As the music gradually diminished, the whistling in my ears returned. I wanted to get up, but couldn't move. Was my physical body dead and permanently immobile? What to do! I possessed a patience I had not known before, and continued to blithely lie there. From a telepathic communication from somewhere in the cosmos, I discovered that I had to readjust my thought vibrations in order to reactivate my physical body. I felt as if I were an assembly plant machine that had been turned off, and now required a warm-up period to begin functioning again.

Everything around me was in a mist of suspension.

Very slowly I took a long, deep breath. Like a clock which begins to tick after it is wound, my body started to rise and fall with the rhythm of my breathing and fresh energies riffled through every cell in my body. I moved my fingers. I wiggled my toes. I was in control. The whistling waned, giving way to the chirping of the birds. I opened my eyes. It was still morning, the aroma of grass still breezing through the window.

Unsteadily, I rolled over to my feet. I was alive, back on the solid planet Earth. Holding on to the walls, I teetered to the boys' bedroom where, as I stood watching them sleep, the whistling in my ears threatened to return. I knew I had to move around to block the vibrations, so cautiously made my way to the kitchen where I walked around sipping coffee until the threat ceased.

I wanted to discuss what had happened with our minister. That evening, Jake stayed with the boys and I drove over to see the Rev. Dr. Peter Morehill. In their comfortable living room, Nancy listened while I answered Peter's slow, deliberate questions. After a while Peter said, "It sounds like you had an out-of-body experience."

Out-of-body experience? As leaders of our study group, Nancy and I had considered ourselves sophisticated in spiritual terminology, but this was new. "The most commonly shared factors are floating above one's body and watching events take place," Peter explained. "Were you frightened?"

"I'm still shaky," I said. "I was frightened when I thought I was dying. All I could think about was how young the boys are, and how much they need a mother."

"When was that?"

"When the body on the bed looked like a statue. I couldn't move."

"You couldn't."

"No, not a muscle. Also, it was sort of scary when it looked as if the ringing in my ears was going to return if I didn't keep moving "

"That can be scary," Peter sympathized. He leaned forward. "Lisa, what was the symphonic music like?"

"Incredible. As if all the orchestras in the world had come together and were performing the Alleluia! Chorus."

"What do you think helped you most to stop being frightened?" Peter smiled.

"When I saw the silver line and thought of an umbilical cord. I don't know why."

"Have you actually seen an umbilical cord?"

"No, I haven't. You know, during delivery they put us completely out. I've probably seen pictures though."

Peter leaned back in his armchair and for a while gazed at the floor, then turning to me said, "Lisa, you're a true mystic."

I didn't want to be a true mystic—whatever that was.

Jake was waiting up when I returned home. "What did Peter say?" he asked.

I sat by his side. "Peter said I was a true mystic. I'm not sure what he means."

"I think it's someone who has mystical experiences."

"Mystical experiences? I thought priests who isolate themselves, or people like St. Augustine, or those who are pronounced saints, are supposed to have mystic experiences. I'm not sure I know exactly what it is. I'm going to look it up," I announced, and brought over the dictionary. "Jake, listen to this. 'From the Greek, *mystikos*: one initiated.' Initiated? I'm not initiated. Initiated into what?"

"Into mysticism?" Jake teased. "I married a sexy mystic."

something using her hands, massaging the parts that hurt. But she was always awake and perfectly normal. Grandma used to gather herbs and make teas with them. Sometimes we'd go with her and she'd tell us what was medicinal and what was not. Then there were things like chamomile and mint which she grew herself. Those teas always made us feel better. God's medicine, she called them."

"There you are Sweetheart, it's in your genes," Jake grinned.

"What's in my genes?"

"Doing things that other people don't understand. Being a Mystic."

I didn't want to be a Mystic—if that meant being different from anyone else. I wanted to be a good wife and mother. I wanted to learn as much as possible about the universe. And, since I hadn't died at 16, I wanted to help others in any way I could.

Later that year Jake was transferred to Chicago, and we settled in a nearby suburb. I discovered the Spiritual Frontiers Fellowship, and met a group of people who were also attempting to interpret paranormal experiences in their lives. We had access to the lending library of the American Society for Psychical Research and I found out about other reported out-of-body cases, and a novel term, *astral travel,* which explained the phenomena of a luminous silvery cord connecting the soul to the physical body. In astral travel, when a subject is asleep or hypnotized, the soul, unaffected by earth's gravity, is able to travel away from the physical body to places not bound by time or space. And, sometimes a person does not have to be asleep to have an out-of-body experience.

I was introduced to another expression: *psychic phenomena.*

At one Society seminar I sensed that an older couple, who appeared to be very devoted to each other, were both watching me intensely. When I'd catch them looking they'd avert their eyes but get back to staring again. During an afternoon break, they ambled over with their arms around each other's waist. She was gray-haired, very thin and tall. He was sturdier, bald, and just about an inch taller. Hesitantly, they introduced themselves and we shook hands. Then in a soft, sweet voice the wife said, "We couldn't help noticing your aura."

They're going to say they're professional psychics I thought, and ask if I want a reading.

"You're a very spiritual person," the man added.

"Thank you," I answered.

After an awkward pause the wife said, "Our son was killed in an automobile accident."

How shocking! All I could manage to say was "I'm sorry." Should I have said, I'm very sorry? Then they'd be reminded of how terrible it was.

"We were wondering . . ." the man hesitated. Standing shoulder-to-shoulder, they now held hands.

"We were wondering," the wife picked up, "if you . . ." and stopped. I studied their glacial faces in pained smiles. "If you," she continued looking intently into my eyes, "had a message for us."

I scanned their calm demeanor, their sad, imploring eyes. I sensed their ardent pain. What kind of a message should I have? I felt so inadequate. "I'm so sorry," I said. "I don't." Their eyes misted, their lips quivered. "I don't have any messages. For anybody. Really."

"That's okay" they said in unison, and the three of us returned to the meeting together.

At another seminar, a man, probably in his 40s, came up to me and, after introducing himself, announced, "You are a Medium."

"Excuse me?"

"You are a Medium," he repeated.

"No, I'm sorry," I hastened, "I'm not." Whatever gave this man that idea? Mediums are weird people who talk to spirits and tap tables and wear veils. Who wants to be that? I'm just an ordinary human being.

"You are," he insisted.

Let's make one thing clear. "I'm not a medium," I insisted back.

"It's in your aura" he said calmly, and strolled away.

One theory accepted by people who believe in an aura is that, just like celestial bodies, the human body also has it's own magnetic atmosphere. This atmosphere, somewhat comparable to ultra-violet light, fluctuates through changes in the person's personality, intelligence, health and spiritual status. Some clairvoyants assert that they are able to discern one's character by analyzing the colors of their aura. The color rose denotes affection. Brilliant red, anger. Muted red, passion and sensuality. Green, healing. Yellow of the purest lemon color, the highest type of intellectual activity. Orange, intellect used for selfish ends, pride and ambition. Gray is associated with depression and fear. Blue indicates religious feeling and spirituality. Purple, psychic ability, spirituality, regal and spiritual power.

In some religious circles, an aura (referred to as a nimbus) is a luminous atmosphere exuding from a god or goddess. In early religious art, an aura was painted around the heads of saints and sacred characters to indicate their sacred personality; later it became known as a halo.

It was at a Society meeting that I met Myrtle R. Walgreen; that Mrs. Walgreen, who, with her husband Charles, had founded Walgreen's Drug Stores. We had an immediate rapport, discussing her autobiography *Never a Dull Day*, specifically the part about an out-of-body experience that Charles had when he was in the army in Cuba. I found Mrs. Walgreen to be a calm, intellectual, gracious, lady, whose major goal at the time was learning about the logistics of psychic phenomena.

It was also through the Society that I learned about documented reports of hearing unusual music when a loved one dies.

Years later, when I was writing on ESP, I received a letter from a reader about such an experience. While vacationing in the Bahamas, one night she and her husband were preparing to go out to dinner. She began to "hear" music. "I knew right away (although I didn't know how I knew) that my mother had just died," she wrote. "Mom hadn't been sick, but I put in a call through to her in Connecticut anyway. We couldn't make the connection, so my husband talked me into going ahead with our dinner plans. When we returned, there was a phone call waiting from my sister. Mom had died unexpectedly. I have never heard that music since."

In the early 1930s, Dr. J. B. Rhine, working with his wife Louisa, headed an innovative field of research termed parapsychology: "Para," to signify that which goes beyond or above accepted psychology. In her 1975 book *PSI: What is it?* Louisa E. Rhine wrote:

> ... Parapsychology is a scientific field, not a cult or "ism" of any kind. It is an attempt to find out the facts about a definite class of phenomena and to do so by carefully controlled experimentation just as the older sciences, like physics and chemistry, biology, and psychology, have established their respective domains.

Dr. Rhine and a colleague in the Duke University Psychology Department, Karl Zener, also popularized an innovative phrase: Extrasensory Perception, dubbed ESP. To substitute for their earlier use of a standard playing-card deck, they created a simple ESP experimentation set of twenty-five cards with five symbols: a square, a circle, a star, three wavy lines and a cross (or plus sign). With the working formula for chance alone established at five correct guesses per run (or 25 percent), any score above that was perceived to show clairvoyance.

After studying the Duke University research, I created my own set of ESP cards and began experimenting. My guesses were not only ten to fifteen correct per run, (at least twice that of chance), but I found that if I put my hand over a card, vibrations of the symbols increased my accuracy. To make the experiments more difficult, I started using a full deck of cards. I was amazed that simply by touch I could tell the difference between red and black—the red felt a lot warmer and sizzling. My score remained close to twice that of chance.

To eliminate the necessity for me to touch each card, I recruited Jake's help. Over and over, my score still remained very comfortably above chance.

Dr. Rhine's easy-to-use cards, originally created for ESP work, are now used in many mainstream instructional elementary mathematics.

Since my out-of-body excursion in 1960, I had learned much. But eighteen years later, the night my sister made her transition, so many questions whirled in my head about that silent, throbbing brilliance.

Chapter 4

Across The Horizon

After Mary's funeral, on my way to the San Francisco airport I noticed that flags were flying at half-staff in honor of former Vice President Hubert Humphrey who had also died that week. And when I got home, it seemed as if all of Minneapolis was abuzz in parades, pageantry and protocol honoring the state's favorite son.

Everywhere people were wrapped up in the loss of this someone so remote to me, not caring that there was a big cavity in my own world. In streets, in shopping malls, in grocery stores, at the library, I had to suppress a compulsion to confront strangers and announce, "Do you know that my sister died?"

It was less than a week after my return when the phone screeched in the lull of midnight, launching me to pounce for the receiver before its second ring. "Yes?" I whispered.

A young girl's voice blurted, "My aunty died."

I didn't recognize the caller. "Just a second," I murmured. "Hold on." Tucking the receiver under the pillow not to awaken Jake, I scurried to the extension in the den. "Who's this?" I asked.

"It's Kim."

"Kim?" I couldn't think of any Kims. "Do you have the right number?"

"Yes."

"Do I know you?"

Like a lost 4-year-old tendering her hand to be trotted home she asserted, "You do now." Kim was 14. She babbled and wailed. A stranger, screaming her pain to the world.

Life took on a normal routine. I resumed leading two spiritual growth studies sponsored by the local Unity church—a Sunday before-service couples group, and a mid-week evening meeting of under-35 singles. To ease the weight of my grief, I concentrated on being thankful that Mary was not suffering any more, envisioning her happy and carefree in that Eden she had profiled.

April was around the corner, soon to usher the rebirth of a long-awaited spring.

Six weeks after Mary's transition, as the sun was beginning to stain the skies orange, I felt someone touch my shoulder as if to say, Wake up. Still groggy, I countered, All right I'm awake. "No," a telepathic connection gently prompted, "you've got to be totally alert."

A web, as if the planet earth had abruptly stopped rotating, infiltrated the cosmos. Don't move, I instructed my psyche, focus on what's happening. Like a slow-motion study of a photograph in the process of being developed, in a codified reverie, a clear image crystallized. And cautiously, I identified a familiar face. It was Mary, who in a mutual flash of recognition, in her natural lilting tone softly said, "Yes, Lisa?"

Yes, Lisa? What do you mean, Yes Lisa? What can I tell you? You're the one who's made the transition. I studied her tranquil demeanor, the dynamism of her gaze. Yes, this was Mary's pure soul that had at one time animated her physical body. Where did she come from? I sensed that, although I was interacting only with her, Mary was not alone; others were instrumental in bringing her to me.

As I was memorizing the contact, Mary's features contorted and she started to weep.

Weep? "Why on earth are you crying?" I asked, baffled.

"I'm sorry," she sobbed.

Chapter 4

"Sorry for what?" Why would she be sorry?

"For putting you through this——" she began, but was cut off. She vanished.

Our communication was in magnetic thought transfer, and her turmoil was intense. I sensed an irritation in me which would well up when Mary sometimes shouldered more than her share of accountability. I knew that her word "you" referred to all of the family, and my reaction was: Why is she affected by our pain when she's finally found peace?

It was vital that I blaze the incident in my memory, so again instructed myself not to move. I didn't budge. She didn't return. The cosmic hush gradually transformed into the rustle of a conforming sunrise on earth. And unable to go back to sleep, mentally I went over every detail of what had just happened, waiting for Jake to wake up.

As was his routine, Jake sprinted out of bed and returned with coffee. "'Morning, Sunshine," he warbled placing the cup on the night stand, leaning over to kiss me. "Thy knave hath brought your morning nectar. What else doth my mistress desire? Tea? Milk? Me? Ready to give."

I was near tears. Reaching for my chin, tenderly he lifted my face. "Are you okay?" he murmured, scooting down by my side as those electric-blue eyes transformed into deep pools of concern. "Sweetheart, are you sick? What's wrong?"

I poured out everything. "I'm the one who should be asking 'Yes Mary, what do you have to tell me?' And why on earth would she cry?"

"She said, I'm sorry?"

"Yes, 'I'm sorry for putting you through this.' Through what?"

He warmed my chilled hands in his. "I expect the bereavement, the grieving."

"It hurt to see her cry. Can you believe this? Here I am, thinking that now she's painless and happy like she said she'd felt that time in a beautiful garden."

"It could be she's apologizing for making the family sad," he said drawing me into his arms.

"Jake?"

"Yes?"

"What do you think it was?"

"I don't know."

"It was so strange. Suddenly she was there, and suddenly she wasn't." I searched his face for answers. "Some people say these things come from the subconscious. If this came from my subconscious, I certainly would've made Mary happy, wouldn't I?"

"It didn't come from your subconscious. It sounds just like Mary, so sensitive to others' feelings." He reached for a cigarette. "How do you know that others brought her?"

"I don't know how I know. There was this non-earthly shush, but the whole scenario was teaming with life, like being in an isolated forest and thinking you're all alone but you're really not. I felt that she didn't make the appearance through her own energies, because when she first talked to me I got the impression she wasn't aware she'd already passed over. She recognized we were on different levels only after saying, 'Yes Lisa?' Maybe because of my surprised reaction to her question."

Parapsychologists agree that many famous psychic visions, and a large proportion of psychic phenomena, happen in the dream state. Some say, because the conscious mind does not filter out messages as it does during the waking state, dreams and telepathic transmissions are a more pure format for communication. Sigmund Freud believed that before the evolution of language, dreams were the normal form of sending and receiving messages and that now, through dreams, the human species simply reverts to this more filtered medium of communication.

In my journal, I recorded:

> When Mary appeared, these were completely unexpected:
> 1) I sensed that Mary had been summoned because I wanted her; much like times on the phone when Mother would say "I'll get your sister," and Mary's first phrase would be, "Hi, Lisa." In this instance, "Yes, Lisa?" was as if someone had said to her, "Lisa wants you" or "Lisa needs to ask a question."
> 2) This encounter could not have been a figment of my imagination or a hallucination, because after expecting some kind of a communication from Mary I had given up, and was beginning to wonder whether survival of consciousness after death was simply wishful thinking by Man.

The memory of Mary's sudden image and weepy disappearance became an aching reality in my daily life. Once in a while Jake would ask, "Have you gotten anything new?" And I'd sigh, "No, nothing."

Mary's birthday in August was coming up. I said to Jake, "I should be with Mother on Mary's birthday, the 25th. I know I was there last year, and with Grace's wedding coming up in October that would make four trips in fifteen months. It'll strain our finances."

"Lisa," he interrupted. "Family comes first. If you think it'll make it a little easier for Mom if you were there, go."

"But . . ."

"Lisa, go. It's the only thing we can do for Mom."

My office okayed a five-day leave-of-absence to be applied toward vacation the following year, and I finalized my travel plans. Then, at the beginning of July, I began to feel Mary's persistent presence, and progressively recognized that there was something new she wanted to communicate to me.

The time had come to face my personal distaste of being labeled "psychic" and to concentrate on becoming a more open pro-active Receiver. But how?

I'd read about, and dismissed, a form of spirit communication through "automatic writing." Originally, it had sounded manipulative and too much like voodoo: a written message occurring without the conscious use of the hand by holding a writing instrument lightly, allowing it free motion. Now the practice loomed as a valid path worth investigating. I turned to my wise, stable spouse. "Jake, do you remember when I found out about automatic writing?" I asked.

"Automatic writing? Yes, I remember your talking about it."

"At the time it seemed weird. Reminded me a lot of using a Ouija board when we were little."

"Didn't you say it didn't move for anyone else? Only when you placed your finger on it?"

"Yes. A hundred years ago, when I was young and carefree."

"You're still young and carefree, Sweetheart."

"I remember we prepared a homemade board with letters. And for a pointer, we'd confiscate a crystal lightweight liqueur glass. When our parents weren't home, we played with it in secret—oh, we were probably about 13 or 14, just us girls. It was scary but fascinating. When the glass moved and stopped at a letter, we'd shout it out and one designated gal wrote it down. We asked questions like, Does so-and-so love so-and-so?"

"And it would say Noooo."

"We didn't have the words YES or NO on the board, it had to spell everything out. So as it sailed toward the letter Y, we giggled and screamed. Whenever I removed my finger from the glass it stopped, and they'd all insist I put my finger back. Teenage stuff!"

"What happened?"

"Our parents found out, and they made us stop."

"Well, you've never tried a modern Ouija board, have you?"

"No Jake, I don't think so. How do I know it wouldn't be me moving it?"
"What about automatic writing?"
"I don't know. Is that any different?"
He hesitated. "Maybe yes, maybe no. You won't find out until you try. It wouldn't hurt, would it?"

I thought of the first time I gleaned that I was aware of things others didn't. I was 5, and often knew what someone else was thinking or sense in advance what they were about to say. And soon discovered two things: one, that it was not socially acceptable to invade others' privacy by tuning in to their thoughts; and two, that I didn't want to be different from others. So, like a pup burying her first bone in the deep secrets of the naked earth, I either didn't share what I knew, or did everything to deny and disregard my intuitions. As I grew up, it was harder and harder for me to reject what others labeled a "sixth sense," and the more I recognized a cosmic commonality, the more altruistic I became with an urgency to grasp the complexities of the universe.

The phenomena of automatic writing is presently explained by two major theories: one, that a "spirit" is manipulating the writing instrument as a written form of communication; two, that the recorded message emanates from one's deep subconscious.

I had to find out what it was that Mary wanted to communicate.

In the middle of July, almost in desperation, I took a spiral notebook and wrote: "Mary, are you here?"

I waited. Nothing. I moved down a few lines, took a couple of deep breaths and cleansing my mind of all outside detractions centered my thoughts on the universality of consciousness. As I watched, the pen lumbered across the page hopping erratically like a Model T-Ford in those old movies. Some forms looked like they could be a letter or word, but I didn't recognize anything. After several pages, discouraged I gave up.

When Jake returned we scanned the pages together. "Lisa," he said, "it could be that your subconscious reluctance is creating some static. In all communication there has to be a compatible transcriber and receiver." Said truly like an engineer, I thought. "Especially in a new form of exchange, a clear playing field is not always immediately possible. Perhaps you should put it away for a while and try again another time."

As August approached, I began to sense geysers of spiritual activities. "What kind of activity do you think it is?" Jake said.

"Some kind of accelerated celestial effervescence, like, you know, when we prepare for the birth of a new baby? Like that. And I'm having persistent nudges that Mary's trying to get in touch with me." Perhaps, I rationalized, it was simply renewed memories of having celebrated Mary's last birthday together. But the stream of ethereal activity avalanched into oceanic proportions and I was certain Mary was involved.

On Sunday morning, August 6, I said to Jake, "I can't ignore this any longer."

"What does it feel like?"

"It's like being in a crowd, and having a child that no-one else sees tugging at your skirt insisting on attention. I've tried to get rid of it but it won't go away. I keep seeing Mary with that innocent sparkle in her eyes and the laughter that used to bubble up. Remember? There's a picture Marc took of the two of us the summer she was in Buffalo. She's wearing her long, pale rose gown, her head thrown back."

"The one on your bookcase."

"Yeah."

"You're both laughing your heads off."

Chapter 4

"Yeah, like that. Can't shake it off. She's so happy."

"Happy. What kind of happiness is it?"

"Gooood question. The closest I can come to it is to say that Mary'd be this happy if she were going to be with Mother again." We stared at each other.

"Could you have had a dream that you can't remember?" Jake nudged.

"I've been concentrating on remembering my dreams." I shook my head. "There's been nothing. But Mary definitely has a message for me."

"Lisa, why don't you try automatic writing again?" he suggested.

I was comfortable with the theory that scientifically unexplained spontaneous experiences labeled "extrasensory perception"—visions, prophetic dreams, mental telepathy—occur because of a change in that person's normal state of consciousness; and that these changed states of consciousness transcend time, space and environment. I still wasn't sure about automatic writing.

"It's worth another try," Jake said. "See how you feel. If it isn't right, you'll know."

"I have to be certain that any messages I get do not come from my subconscious," I emphasized. "Can I still my conscious mind enough to allow this type of communication?"

"Of course you can" Jake encouraged, and kindled by his recent acquisition of an instrument pilot's license took off for a scheduled flight in his beloved skies. As the day waned into a postcard-peaceful evening, my passion to understand got stronger and stronger.

With paper and pen, I eased into a chair at our dining room table. To quiet my mind, I did deep breathing exercises. To quiet my apprehensions, I affirmed "I let go (of all anxieties), and let God (the all good)." To still my psyche, I visualized a placid lake where, floating on my back, the sun bathed my face sifting through to my soul, and the blends of honeysuckle and oleander breezed by from shore. This was the end-of-class relaxation technique I used for my yoga students. Now at ease, alert and ready I wrote:

"Mary, do you want to tell me something?"

Nothing happened. I moved the pen to another location and waited again. In a minute or two, the pen skipped around in spastic jumps. Then, as if controlled by a central magnet, it made full circles, retracing over and over each outline in a smooth, satiny counter-clockwise direction. As I watched each circle thicken, I knew I personally did not have the artistry of that steady accuracy.

I moved to another page, and soon recognized the word *"Mother,"* followed by *"and I are going to be together."*

Then, *"Go to Mother and tell her we are always going to be together. Love and kisses. Give my love to the boys."*

I studied the writing. Clearly, this had to be the end of the message because Mary had always signed her letters "love and kisses."

That night I pointed out to Jake, "Here, see, 'going to be together.' What does this mean? And here at the end, 'Give my love to the boys.' If this came from my subconscious, believe me, the boys were the farthest thing from my mind."

"Mary loved the boys, that's for sure."

"When I'm doing it, I feel as if I'm in a different world."

"How?"

"As if I'm having a dream while completely awake. Sort of transported into a deeper consciousness."

"Are you aware of things around you?"

Chapter 4

"Very much so, but completely detached."

"Do you still feel that Mary's very happy?"

"Yes. Even more so. Something's making her very happy. And, a whole group of people are getting ready for the arrival of a big head of state. I wish I knew what."

"I think you'll know," Jake said in his usual calm manner. My endearing Jake, always there, always my rock.

Next morning when I picked up the newspaper with the headline "Pope Paul VI Dies of Heart Attack" I raced to Jake. "Look at this. I must have been picking up activities for the transition of a spiritual leader. It's the Pope."

"Yeah, that's it. It has to be," he mused. "But Lisa, you also said that Mary was very happy."

"Yes."

"Mary wasn't a Roman Catholic," he reminded me. "And you got the word, Mother."

A few days later a letter from Greg read:

> My dearest Lisa,
>
> A short note to let you know how much I appreciate your concern about Mother and me and the rest of the family, and your proposed visit during the week of Mary's birthday.
>
> Since you're coming in October for Grace's wedding, there's no need for you to make another short trip now. Instead, why not come for the wedding a week before Jake and the boys, then we can have some extra time together.
>
> I'll try to take Mother out of the house for a few days during the week of the 25th—probably Fresno or somewhere else.
>
> With love and warm kisses, Greg

I was in a dilemma. Greg's solution was sensible. But I couldn't dismiss the ever-present nudge to go back and spend more time with Mother.

"Why don't you go anyway?" Jake said.

"Sweetheart, it isn't that simple. It's Greg's house. How can I insist? The week of Mary's birthday is going to be very tough for Mother, but who am I to tell Greg what we should do? He thinks he can handle the situation without me." So with trepidation, I canceled my airline reservations.

Mother and I talked by phone several times a week. Once, her voice crinkling across the lines, she confided, "Mary was my youngest and needed me. Lisa, I'm not able to handle it. I'm lost. I miss her so very, very much."

"Mother, don't you see her in your dreams?"

"Yes, my sweet daughter. It's my only consolation," she whimpered.

As the time for Mary's birthday got closer, in spite of Greg's reassuring letter, in the rhythm of all my senses I heard the quiver of an ongoing disturbance around Mother. "Something's not right in San Francisco," I told Jake.

"What?"

"I don't know. Something they're not telling me about."

"You talk to them all the time," he said.

"That doesn't mean they tell me everything. Greg's so unreasonably protective, shielding women from bad news unless absolutely necessary."

One evening I couldn't stand it any longer, and contacted Valerie. "How's Mother doing now?" I tried to sound casual.

"She's better," Valerie replied. "Her arm is beginning to get more feeling."

I had no idea what she was talking about, but to glean more I said, "Oh, that's good."

"Well, her numbness didn't last long anyway," Val continued. "In a short time she started to use it more and more."

What numbness? And what's a short time? Trying not to hoist a red flag I asked, "What's the latest from her doctor?"

"He said he couldn't be sure. It could have been a mild stroke."

Chapter 4

"I forget what side it was," I egged her on.

"Oh, it was on her left side, and it affected only her left arm." Valerie had no idea she was giving me hidden information. "She says she's still a little weak in that part, but she seems to be doing quite well. You know how Mama's always been. Still insists on doing everything herself."

Not to alarm Valerie, I said, "Things like that can sometimes be a pinched nerve which affects a limb," adding, "I forget, did she have pain?"

"No, it suddenly went numb. She said there was no pain at all."

My knees wobbled, but I kept my voice steady. "Does she have pain now?"

"No, Mama says that it's as if there are prickling needles up and down her arm. Like electricity."

"All the time?"

"All the time. Not on and off."

I immediately dialed Mother. She gave me details willingly, saying her arm was feeling more normal every day. "Why didn't you tell me, Mom?"

"Oh, we didn't want to worry you," she said. "What can you do out there?"

Two days later I called again. The phone rang and rang. I was going to hang up when Mother came on the line. She didn't appear alert. "Were you sleeping, Mom?" It was before noon their time.

"No." She hesitated. "You know. Well . . ."

"What, Mother?"

"My daughter. Well——" she cut herself off.

"Mother, what?" I urged.

"Nothing. Nothing, my sweet daughter."

"Are you feeling okay, Mom?"

"Yes."

"Is your arm still tingling?"

"It isn't my arm."

"What Mom? What?"

She hesitated. "Nothing. Are you and Jake well? Are the boys well?"

I couldn't coax her to tell me anything more.

The next day I called at their dinner time. No one answered. I tried Greg at the office. He wasn't there. Alarmed, I dialed Valerie. "I talked to them last night," she said. "Believe me, there wasn't anything unusual."

"Please Valerie, would you try to locate them and get back to me?"

"Lisa, is something wrong? Are you picking up anything?"

"No, no," I lied.

Early the next morning, Valerie apologized, "It was late last night, so I didn't call back."

"Valerie, what's going on?"

"Mama was hospitalized yesterday."

"When?"

"That's where they were when you called. Greg took her in. They think she may have had another stroke."

My body was shaking like a leaf in a tornado. "How bad is it?"

"It's going to be all right," Valerie reassured me. "Greg says, they're going to let her come home today. So, you see, they must think she's going to be okay." No, I didn't see that. I was angry they'd made me cancel my trip.

Mother was released that afternoon. As Greg was carrying her upstairs she collapsed, and was readmitted to the hospital.

Chapter 4

The next morning, Sunday, I woke Valerie up. "Mama's doing fine," she reported. "Last night we were all there. Don't worry Lisa, when we were leaving she kissed all of us good night."

I told Jake, "I wish I could be as calm as they are. Something's very wrong."

On Monday, I could hardly wait for my lunch break to call. After counting twelve rings, I was about to give up when Valerie answered. It was 9:00 o'clock there. "What's going on?" I demanded. "You told me you'd call if something changed. I know something has."

"I got home this minute," Valerie panted.

"Tell me what's happening."

"Lisa, listen to me. Mama went into a coma last night."

Chapter 5

Other Places

In the morning, again, as I'd done seven months earlier, I boarded the ten-thirty flight to San Francisco where Greg was pacing at our arrival gate. "I know Mother will be glad you're here," he said. "The doctors tell us her heart is strong." On the ride to the hospital, Greg chattered away as I kept searching his face. Why did I sense that Mother wasn't with us. Was he keeping it from me, or didn't Greg know she was already gone? Or, perhaps, I reasoned, in a universal zone being in a coma was the same as not being here.

"Mother's strong," Greg emphasized. "You wouldn't believe it. That first evening when her arm went numb, you should have seen her. I was watching the news after dinner and I heard this big clang in the kitchen, and a long moan. I rushed in and found her at the sink looking down at a platter that had cracked. She said, 'Son, I don't feel anything in my arm.' I wanted us to go to the hospital immediately, but she kept insisting she wouldn't budge until she'd finished cleaning up. The place was immaculate when we left."

Speeding by California's towering redwoods along thoroughfares with medians landscaped in lush sycamores, we pulled into the hospital parking lot and in a swift elevator climbed to the fourth floor.

Valerie and a close friend Bev Sharian were standing outside Mother's room obviously waiting for our arrival, and as soon as our eyes met Val stepped forward and grabbed me in a welcome hug. When I started to pull away to go into Mother's room she tightened her hold. In my peripheral vision, I caught a glimpse of Bev holding back a squirming Greg.

"I want to see Mother now," I said, trying to twist out of Val's arms. She gripped me closer, as straining back I shrugged "Let me go."

"Oh my dear." Valerie held my face in both her hands and gazed into my eyes as tears surged down her pale cheeks.

"I've got to see her" I whimpered, knowing it was too late. Mother's heart had stopped at noon, the exact hour my plane landed. And on Mary's birthday, August 25, at 1:30 p.m., Mother's physical body was lowered alongside her youngest daughter. Up there on the windy hill by San Francisco Bay.

The day after the funeral, at mid-afternoon I had stretched out on the sofa in the living room while Valerie and Grace with Allen (who had flown from Chicago to attend his grandmother's funeral), had gone shopping for groceries. Greg, exhausted from all the activities, was taking a nap in his bedroom. It was disorienting being in that house without Mother's potent presence.

I remembered the time I was 6. More than anything in the whole world, I yearned for a delicate porcelain doll like the ones my friends with wealthy fathers had. Imported from England, she was 9" tall and came in her own white cardboard box with a lid and was very, very expensive—way beyond my single, working mother's budget. On New Year's Day (a festive gift-giving celebration for Armenians), after we were all decked out in our holiday finery, Mother handed out our presents. When it came my turn, with a smile that started at the corners of her mouth spreading to her chiseled high-cheekbones, Mother offered that magical white box which cradled a doll more dazzling than my fantasies. She had a mane of cascading bronze curls, peaches-and-cream complexion, and thick chestnut lashes which, like a velvet curtain, hid her limpid blue eyes when you laid her down. Her pale pink taffeta party gown was trimmed with lace at the neckline and the hems of her short ruffled skirt and puffed sleeves. On her feet she wore the daintiest of white dancing slippers topped with matching bows.

The doll and I had been mother-and-daughter for two days when the family was having afternoon tea on the veranda and, very proud of my new stature, I perched on a high raffia stool cooing and rocking my miracle from heaven. As I scrambled down to reach for a cookie, the doll slipped from my lap shattering on the concrete into a thousand cracks. What hurt most was the depth of the cloud in my mother's eyes as she knelt beside me to gather the pieces. And she didn't scold me. I felt guilty. I felt crushed. I cried only at night when no-one could see me. About two weeks later on a Sunday afternoon, I was playing soccer with the boys (always designated as a goalie), when Mother summoned me during a break. Inside, caressing my tussled sunstreaked brown hair away from my wet forehead, she handed me a white box. "Here, take good care of your doll," she whispered.

Now, recalling that little girl, I smiled at the unforgettable lessons Mother had taught us by example. Except for the whir of the refrigerator from the kitchen, the house was silent. Emotionally and physically exhausted I began yoga relaxation, visualizing a oneness with the energies of the cosmos and a peace with universal intelligence.

My eyes were closed, my breathing rhythmic, my mind still. I was drifting into sleep, when I heard Mary's voice—soft and soothing. It seemed very natural for her to be speaking to me in her own home. The communication appeared to be from the space just above where I was lying down. Her voice droned on and I had trouble understanding her. I knew she was explaining something. What?

As I focused on absorbing the contact, like a special-effects overlay there appeared an image of one of Mary's dresses which was still hanging in her bedroom closet: a straight-line, daffodil-yellow linen with white leather pockets, which she'd bought just before returning home from a vacation with us in Buffalo, and wore for her flight back West.

"Do you remember that day I left you to return home?" Mary's voice now came through clearly. "Remember how sad you were?" I remembered.

"Remember how my family was waiting for me, and how happy they were when they met me at the airport, and we had a party when we got home?" I remembered.

"Well, that's the way it is with what we call death. You're sad because Mother left. We here have been waiting for her arrival joyfully. It's like preparing for the birth of a new baby."

I thought of that August 6th when I couldn't ignore how happy she had seemed to be. "Is that what your joy was about that Sunday," I asked. "You were so elated?"

"Yes," Mary replied. "They had just told me that Mother was coming." (She didn't identify who "they" were. I thought "they" had to be the ones who had been caring for her.)

Mary's smile was radiant. Standing beside her was Sport, who had died three years earlier. He had that pleased expression, the "here I am" look whenever he muzzled himself into a family group. I recalled that day Mary was leaving: Sport wouldn't let her get in the passenger's seat where he had parked himself. I had to get out of the car, go over and peel him off.

I wondered where Mother was, and in an instantaneous thought transmission, was told that I couldn't see her because it was "too soon." What that meant, I wasn't sure. Later, I learned that some believe there is a seventy-two-hour "block-out" period following physical death. Much like not being accessible when traveling on the dark side of the moon.

With that, Mary's image went into a long, slow fade-out as if it were the end of a presentation, again, like a reverse process of a photograph now vaporizing into the ethers. I drifted back into the earth's nurturing womb of time and space, gradually allowing my eyes to open.

Although Mary's contact didn't feel unnatural, I was amazed to see Sport in his devil-may-care stance. The first year our boys were away in college, every weekday afternoon Sport kept vigil at the picture window for their return home from high school. And one morning, when our silver Mercury sedan was sailing away with a Salvation Army driver at the wheel, sitting at my feet he, too, waved a teary good-bye to a family member.

Now, I heard the others returning home and rose to open the door before they rang the doorbell. "Mom, you'll never believe this," Allen said. "Wait till you see the size of California artichokes. Aunt Val says Grandma loved them."

With Grace's wedding scheduled less than six weeks away, Richard and Val were in a dilemma. Following a death in the family, the Armenian Orthodox Church sanctions a forty-day mourning period of no music and festivities. Although the wedding date cleared this dedicated time-frame, showers and festive parties were planned for the interim period. "What are we going to do Aunty?" Grace asked. "Dad is insisting that all our pre-wedding parties be canceled."

Tradition is a very important part of Armenian culture; especially religious traditions. "Give yourselves time," I suggested. "Think perhaps about not making a decision for a while and see how you feel in a couple of weeks."

As we rolled once more to catch my flight to Minneapolis, I noticed flags flying in celebration of the election of a new Pope—John Paul I, who, it turned out, was destined to serve only thirty-four days.

On our drive home from the airport, I said to Jake "Who would have thought I'd never see Mother alive again when I kissed her good-bye in January."

Chapter 5

"Lisa," he said softly. "After you left, I picked up your notebook and went over your automatic script. There is one place where it clearly reads 'Mother and I are going to be together.' That, to me, meant at the same plane."

"I didn't want to believe it. And, because I wanted to be sure that the writing was not from my own subconscious, I went overboard in denying it was a specific instruction. I knew 'Go to Mother' was clear, but Greg said don't come."

Jake took my hand. "I know."

"And, I didn't want to insist that I go. They would have started asking me questions."

"I know Sweetheart" he agreed, pulling my hand to his lap.

This was my soul mate of unfaltering wisdom. In Africa, after I'd gotten to know him, there was no question in my mind that he was the man I wanted to marry. With the rising probability of my flying away to that continent which, to Mother, might as well have been on the moon, she once hesitated, "Why don't you marry Tony? He's here, he comes from a highly respected family, he's already established. And, you'll live like a queen for the rest of your life."

"I don't love Tony, Mother," I reminded her.

"Well, you'll learn to love him. He's so good to you," she pointed out. Tony was good to me and I was flattered by his month-after-month persistence. But in addition to being knockdown leading-hero gorgeous, I had glimpsed Jake's soul. Jake was what I needed.

Now, back home in Minnesota, it was a week after Mother's death. I woke up from a deep sleep sensing that something or somebody was trying to get my attention. "You know this person well," the cosmos signaled. I concluded it had to be Mother trying to tell me something—it was her personality, her entity. She was in the ethers and I was here on the planet earth, and identifying someone in the ethers wasn't easy. This must have been the way Jesus appeared to the two women at the graveside, I thought, and that's why they couldn't be sure; no wonder they mistook him for the gardener.

I started drifting back to the planet earth and waking up. Deliberately, I willed myself back into the cosmos. In a few seconds, the vision restarted like a movie that had been temporarily halted. It *was* Mother and she was intent on making me understand something very important to her. I tried. And tried. I couldn't figure what she wanted me to know. I fell asleep.

In the morning I felt strange—detached—still caught up in a foreign universe as I drove to work feeling like an alien on Earth. I had just made a left turn onto a busy highway and was picking up speed when I sensed a charged atmosphere in the car. It seemed as if the vehicle had become enveloped in a foreign electrical current. Stay in control, I told myself, it's going to be all right. Again I felt Mother's presence. I turned the radio off. "No, no, no," I heard a voice, with Mother's tone and inflection. "Absolutely not." Whenever Mother was really adamant about us taking her *no*'s seriously, she'd always say it three times—no, no, no! I wanted to take my hands and cover my ears to shut out whatever it was that wouldn't leave me alone. I knew I couldn't stop the vibes so I gave in: Okay, okay, What is it?

I heard Mother's voice. "Don't any of you make foolish decisions. I want my granddaughter to have everything exactly as planned for her wedding. Why should my sweet grandchild have to give up what she's entitled to? Keep happy traditions. Celebrate joy."

How can a mere mortal tell if this is really Mom's message, or something from somewhere deep within my subconscious? Should I ignore it? Should I contact Rich and Grace?

When I got home Jake suggested, "Why don't you do automatic writing and see?"

"You think so?"

"I think so."

Chapter 5

"I'm not sure that's really any different. Any different than my subconscious, I mean."

"When you wrote down that message from Mary, you didn't even know that your mother had had a stroke. Lisa, how could it have been from your subconscious?"

"Yeah, I realize that. But Jake, where does all this come from?"

"What does it matter, Lisa? You're always so skeptical. That's why I looked at the writing when you were in San Francisco after Mom died. It was correct, wasn't it?"

"I know. I just want to be sure that all this is not in my mind."

"Wherever it's coming from, it's proven to be right. It's you, Lisa. You communicate with the trees. You talk to the birds. Stray cats and neighbors' pets come over and you carry on a conversation. You tell me all things on the planet are alive and interactive."

"Yeah, they sure are. Doesn't everybody know that? Don't you?"

He smiled, shaking his head. "Not the way you do, Sweetheart. You remember telling me how at the office Gail thought you were nuts when you got excited about your plant sprouting leaves?"

"Yeah. Everybody thought the plant was dead and wanted me to throw it away. I wouldn't, because I knew it was still alive. One day I saw that it had sprouted leaves. Gail came over and said to me," I lowered my voice, "'Lisa, your life must be very dull if you can get that excited about a dead plant sprouting leaves.'" We both chuckled. "There is a bond between all life, animate and inanimate. And the universe is connected."

"Well then, automatic writing has to be just one form of communication within the universal connection. Sweetheart, that was only your second time with automatic writing. Eventually, you'll feel more comfortable about it. I think you should do it."

"You think so?"

"I know so. When you first started, the writing began with meaningless lines, symbols and circles. As you practiced, it smoothed out. Every new skill is perfected through trial and error. Even a child falls down many times before learning to walk."

I thought and thought and thought about it. Jake was so right. And I did need to make sense out of Mary's first tearful appearance.

With pen and notebook, I retreated to my favorite sofa in the den. Like a preset planet with a gravitational pull, the pen went into elliptical circles in a magnetic counter-clockwise direction. Then, as if the spheres were merely a warm-up exercise, before I had time to pen the question in my mind, Why were you crying when you appeared to me that first time? it began:

"I was sorry I put everyone through all that sorrow."

This sounded so much like Mary when she was in her physical body. I'd thought death would have made her less concerned about other people's hurts; it looked like it hadn't. I proceeded:

"When you told me about Mother, it was August 6 here. She went into a coma on the 20th and died on Tuesday the 22nd. When did you know? And who told you?"

"I knew that day. I don't know what day it was because we do not have days like you. The angels here told me."

"Is that what you were trying to tell me?"

"Yes, I wanted you to know that I was going to meet her soon."

"When did you know that you yourself were going to go over?"

"The day you called and Greg said that I was better. It was New Year's Eve. I didn't want to spoil everyone's

Chapter 5

holiday. Then I became very sick . . . I agreed to be taken to the hospital to help Mother and Greg.

"I was ready to go but didn't want to make everyone sad. When you came to the hospital you knew, and I could finally leave."

The phraseology, the feelings, the concern for others; it all sounded so much like the Mary we all knew. I was mesmerized. I asked whether she remembered how she went over, and about the light in my room, and that I expected her to come to me in person.

"I did come over but I was too weak. God's presence filled your room. And you woke up. I had made the transition before I left my physical body. When the doctors said they suspected brain damage, I was not there any more."

(Brain damage? I hadn't known about brain damage. I suspected Greg and Richard had protected us women from that information.)

"Was it painful for you?"

"No it was not painful. It was beautiful once I went over. The angels helped me. And I was really very happy until they brought me to you that night."

"Were you there with us as a family during the preparations, and funeral?"

"No. We were not there because I could not bear to see all of you so sad."

"Who do you mean by We?"

"The angels. We are always together. They love me and help me here."

"What about when Mother went over?"

> "We were waiting for her here, and when she went into the coma, we helped her over. It was very peaceful. She came willingly. She knew me right away and then my father met her and we were happy we were together. She was so sweet and loving. They all love her here."

Mary, talking about how everyone loves her mother, just like she did when she was in her physical body.

Once I recorded:

> "I want to be positive that what I write is the Truth and not just something that has come from me as a person."
>
> "Truth is universal. Love is universal. Death is not the end; it is really the beginning of the universal love consciousness drawing unto itself that which is a part of the whole."
>
> "Are there spirits who wait for you when you are going to make the transition?"
>
> "Yes. Spirits show you where you are and give you help to adjust to your new place."

In using the word "help," it appeared that when souls first pass through the physical veil of death, they start from a new beginning, and because it is a foreign environment they need to adapt in the same manner as an immigrant becomes acclimated to an unfamiliar way of life. That's why familiar entities greet them and help with their adjustment.

> "Was it a beautiful garden like you told me that other time?"
>
> "Yes. It is very beautiful."
>
> "What are you doing there?"
>
> "We are growing."
>
> "What is physical death?"

Chapter 5

"It is a fulfillment of the soul as it grows toward perfection."
"Are you happier now?"
"Yes. And I know everything you do."
"What about angels?"
"Angels are always with you and they protect you. They are with the same person either here or there."
"Can you tell me more about angels"
"Yes. We walk before you and protect you. Angels are here but work with people on earth to help them in their lives. Very much like Jesus."

At that time I didn't believe in angels. I used to think that adults spoke of them as they speak of fairies. Later, when Jake and I were going over the writings I said, "That makes sense, doesn't it? It would explain how the teachings of different prophets help different groups of believers. One draws unto oneself the spiritual entity who'll help them most at that period in their evolutionary process."

On November 21, 1978, the world went into shock with news of the Guyana carnage. I wanted to find out why there is so much hurt from one human being to another. I asked: "Mary, what is the spiritual explanation of that religious sect in Guyana committing mass murder and suicide? Are they with you now?" The pen circled for quite a while until, slowly, it simply wrote:

"Our duty is to love and cherish every soul."

One night I had a dream with Mary in it. The next day Val called to say that she had had a very vivid dream of Mary who looked so healthy and so beautiful. In my automatic writing I asked if she could be with Val and me at the same time, or whether it was just a coincidental dream?

> *"I was with both of you. You don't see me with your physical eyes because I am in a different body made of some light that does not have material form. It is like the rays of the sun that you cannot see by themselves."*
>
> "Is our new body then made of a substance like light? Like the light that I saw when you made your transition?"
>
> *"Yes."*
>
> "Do you communicate like electrical connections?"
>
> *"Love connections."*

Often, the answers were not what I expected. Most of the time, when Mother came through in automatic writing, I was completely unprepared. At times Mother appeared and wrote in Armenian when I really wanted to continue in English with my sister. And many times I'd get communication from Mother about the dramatic cornucopia of flowers everywhere, when I was anxious to get through to Mary with more urgent questions.

In a television documentary about Einstein's life and his scientific discoveries, I noticed that a lot of the forms which the commentator outlined and used on the board were startlingly similar in shape to elliptical forms created during the beginnings of automatic writing. In another documentary, I watched in mesmerized fascination as planetary movements were traced in counter-clockwise elliptical directions. I recorded in my journal: "Will there some day be a scientific explanation for this form of communication, which duplicates elliptical planetary movements?"

The energy flow which moved my writing element functioned more and more efficiently with each use.

Chapter 5

As Christmas was approaching, one day I'd been sensing the presence of Mother and Mary very strongly. I had to see if I could make graphic contact.

In the evening, Jake was participating in a year-end racquetball tournament in our complex. A silvery, sub-zero Minnesota night shimmered outside, as I got my writing pad and pen to see if I could make a graphic contact. It took me only a few minutes to still my mind and concentrate on the blank page.

"Dearest sister, do you know what is going to happen on earth in advance? If so how long in advance?"

"Yes, we know what will happen before you do, but I don't know how far in advance. We do not have time here."

"What is it like out there now when the calendar is going to begin over and we add a digit to the year? What goes on?"

"Time is on earth. We know you live in time and we work with you. We help you with your testing and life challenges.

I wondered how Christmas, the most joyful of all Christian holidays, was celebrated in the spiritual realm. Mary's answer:

"We celebrate every day with joy and love and good will to every man."

"Are there special days at all?"

"Yes. Our special days are when they come here. We celebrate their birth."

Grace's pre-wedding festivities were held as originally scheduled. She had asked me to participate in an Armenian tradition that only a happily married woman positions the bride's headdress in place. And, just before she walked down the aisle, I anchored Grace's exquisite ivory lace headband embroidered in seeded pearl, with yards and yards of wispy white veil encircling her beautiful glowing face.

And we all knew that Mother was smiling.

What we didn't know, was that my most portentous cosmic connection was still ahead.

Chapter 6

Adrift

Barely two months after the wedding, I received a letter from Grace reflecting the shock that once again reverberated throughout the United States:

> The radio is on. A news flash. Mayor Moscone and Supervisor Harvey Milk have been shot by Dan White, another supervisor. Both are dead.
> I can't believe it. The world is going crazy. What's happening to people? Violence, murder, Jonestown, San Francisco. The pressures are mounting; the questions are getting out of control; the answers more and more obscure. It's insane.
> The Jonestown horror left me curiously unmoved. My own lack of reaction was more frightening to me than the mass suicides. But where the deaths of 900 people didn't reach me, the murder of two has settled into my bones and frozen the marrow. It's not frightening—it's terrifying. There's terror in the inability of people to cope with life.

On the evening of Thursday, November 30, saddened by a world that appeared in total turmoil, I watched Mayor Moscone's funeral on television. And like others, I, too, wept as their family priest walked up to the podium and gently guided the Mayor's daughter, who had barely gotten through her shaky eulogy. I wanted to heal every wound, I wanted to put my arms around every member of those grieving families and dilute their despair.

I remembered being in San Francisco during the mayoral elections when Greg had sat up late into the night for the final tally. Now I went to bed hurting by the chasm in my own life carved by the death of a sister and mother within a seven-month span. I wondered, had Mary prematurely tossed aside her own will to survive? That last Christmas, when she told me how severe the symptoms of their colds were, I said, "You'll all be well for New Year's." Softly she'd answered, "We'd better." What did that mean? Had she given up too soon? What was too soon? How could anyone but Mary know her struggle and suffering.

I had fallen asleep to the rhythm of these questions skating in my head, when a haunting hush whirled me awake. I knew I was safe and in my bedroom. As I promised myself I would remember, a series of events began to unfold like a classical epic.

In a maternal aura, far, far away from the planet Earth, not wanting to burden the family with her diminishing health, Mary had left home. Although no one had specifically told me I was sure she wasn't around any more. (It reminded me of Mary's first hospitalization. I'd said to Jake, "I don't think Mary's home." "What makes you say that? Wouldn't they tell you if she weren't?" "No, they wouldn't. You know how overly protective they are with women." It was only after I called to specifically ask, was I told that Mary was in the hospital undergoing tests.)

Now, in that sixth dimension, I was determined to find my sister and bring her back. A vehicle approached and stopped just long enough for me to hustle in. It was driven by someone I didn't know, with others in the car, also all strangers, launched on a search for Mary. I sensed the driver was a designated person who specialized in this kind of mission, and was comfortable with the supportive presence of the others. Smoothly, as if floating on ice, we began to coast on a deserted highway.

In the horizon I glimpsed a small entity cross the road from the left to the right shoulder, and undeterred, persevere on her individual journey in the same direction as we were traveling. Pointing at the figure, I shouted "There she is," jumping up and down on my seat like a toddler in day-care who catches sight of

Chapter 6

a parent. "Slow down, slow down," I begged. In a lingering airplane-like motion, the car glided to the side of the moving figure as, in one sweep, I reached over and lifted the featherweight figure into the vehicle draping her on my lap. And like a silk scarf I sheathed her body with my own, cradling her head and snuggling close to her pale and weary face.

It was Mary. Gazing at me she confided, "I tried. I really tried." And, in rhythm to the universal pulse in which we were engulfed, I signaled "I know, I know."

"There were so many people telling me to come," Mary explained. "'Come on over. Come on over,' they kept repeating. It was as if once I started I couldn't stop from continuing my journey."

"It's all right," I reassured her, then eased back to identify this entity accurately. Yes, it was Mary. Her pasty face looked dead, but the animating energy which was once a loving human being I knew as my sister shone through like a rainbow in the mist. A solemn peace blanketed everything. And I knew she had made her transition.

I must return to earth I said to myself, and was re-submerged into our planet's nucleus where again I could not immediately animate my physical body. Calmly I waited. Drip by drip, like a vessel coming alive, my lungs began to fill with air and fresh oxygen actuated every cell in my physical body. After a couple of breaths, I rolled over to my left side. If I return onto my back, will the communication continue? I rolled back, feeling the downy crush of my pillow under my neck. Nothing happened; I remained on the planet earth. I looked over at the clock. It was 12:30. Jake continued to sleep.

I got out of bed, went into the living room, strolled in circles, picked up a book and curled in an armchair began reading. But nothing registered. Promising myself that I would remember and record every detail of my odyssey, I returned to bed and fell asleep in the hush of pre-dawn.

Later, through my research I found that sometimes when a person dies without having had the opportunity of saying a formal good-bye, or leaving without having said something important they had wanted to say, there have been these types of encounters.

For thousands and thousands of years, way before Freud popularized the discussion of dream interpretation in academia, ancient Egyptians, Greeks and primitive cultures were trying to understand the universal experience of dreams.

In the industrialized world, inventors, artists and even political leaders have credited their insights to observations in dreams. Paul C. Fisher, creator of the space pen carried on manned space flights, has openly talked about seeing his company's first product in a dream. It is said that President Lincoln dreamed of his assassination, Harry Truman had a dream that F.D.R. had died, catapulting him into the presidency, and President Lyndon Johnson decided not to run for reelection after a dream. A dream is credited for composer Igor Stravinsky's "Rite of Spring," and the discovery of the structure of the benzene molecule. The pre-Romanesque church and monastery, Mont St. Michel, is believed to have been conceived through a series of dreams. A successful designer and owner of a promotional gift company launched in the mid 1980s on the West Coast, attributes a great deal of her business success and problem-solving answers to her dreams, which she jots down in explicit detail—colors, curves, lines. And there are innumerable undocumented cases of dreams which have opened doors to creative activities.

Researchers are now beginning to concur that dreams can even be an early warning system for illness. And, initially proposed by Harvard neurophysiologist J. Allan Hobson in 1988, more and more scientists now agree that the chemistry of the awake brain is different than during sleep.

Chapter 6

In the 1990s, PET scanning, a scientific process that monitors brain activity by taking a series of pictures every 10 minutes, began to open many new doors to formerly unknown brain activities, pinpointing the brain's deep structures that regulate thinking and emotions, and surface regions that process sights and sounds. Researchers can now graphically identify such emotions as fear—when a red glow erupts from the structure known as the amygdala; and the reconstruction of a long-buried telltale memory—when specific neurons begin to fire rapidly. It is established that the brain of the human species has a specialized region for processing emotional perceptions and memories, and many scientists believe that emotion is central to the process of rational thought.

In analyzing a dream, it is important to separate brain activity which may be getting rid of debris, from a genuine altered state of consciousness with a specific message. Often this occurs only after a great deal of soul searching, studying and research and work at remembering our dreams.

In Minneapolis, a young couple in their late twenties, Christine a registered nurse, and her husband Bob a medical student, were members of a spiritual growth group I led.

One Sunday, Christine asked me if we could talk in private. After we settled together on a sofa, she said, "I'd like to tell you about a dream. It was five years ago, but it has now come back to haunt me."

"Okay."

"It was Sunday night, early Monday morning. I dreamed that Jennifer, my younger sister, was ill and was taken to the doctor. The diagnosis was lung cancer."

"Is this all in your dream?"

"Yes, all in my dream. I was watching my parents and Jennifer getting her stuff into her car to go to the hospital. I was busy with my life and didn't know what to say or do for anyone, so I just sat back and watched, feeling upset." Christine fidgeted, changed her position on the sofa, then continued: "They took Jennifer's dresser because it seemed she was never going to come out of the hospital again." I reached over and held her hand.

Christine was calm. "All through the dream I was very upset and extremely angry at God for letting such a thing happen to my sister. She was only 17-years-old at the time."

"This was five years ago?"

"Really. But it has come back to me as if it were yesterday. Do you know why?"

"No, why?"

"On Tuesday afternoon, Jennifer called. She said that she had had a persistent cough and had gone to see the doctor. The X-rays were abnormal. She had strange white spots all along the medial surfaces of her lungs spreading outward. They took blood tests which takes a week. I about fell off my chair when Jennifer told me all this and I felt numb, but I tried to sound normal as we chatted a few more minutes. And now I just can't get that dream out of my mind."

Jennifer was hospitalized that week. Christine said to me, "You know Lisa, my dream experience has now returned to me so vividly I'm able to return to it at will."

One evening, when I knew she wasn't there, I called Bob and explained that Christine's dream was a precognitive message that Jennifer will be dying.

"Do you think I should tell her?" he asked.

"Perhaps not outright," I said. "You may at first want to make sure she knows you're there for her. Maybe making it easy for her to spend as much time as she wants with her sister and family. Things like that."

"Of course," Bob agreed. "Shouldn't I refer to the dream at all?"

"I think it's wise not to take all hope away. Let her make her own conclusions, knowing you're listening and understand. And we know that, although it is very painful for us, the answer to complete healing sometimes occurs through transition."

Jennifer was confirmed with inoperable lung cancer, and released to return home to spend her last days with the family. One evening Christine called. "Spiritually, I'm at peace," she told me, "but emotionally I'm shaking and almost ill. The incongruence of my upset emotions and my peaceful spiritual self makes me ashamed that I have so little faith."

"You know Christine, it's okay. Usually both are present during this kind of shock, regardless of faith."

When Christine called again, she said "Lisa, Jennifer has definitely crossed the highway."

"What makes you say that?"

"If you look into her eyes she's no longer there, she's gone. It's just her physical body that is functioning. I don't think that she can cross the road back at this time." It reminded me of Mary crossing that road.

A week later Christine confessed, "It's been very rough. Jennifer is now almost in a coma. But, you wouldn't believe it. She's fighting all the way, talking a blue streak."

"What's she saying?"

"Her words are slurred, and I don't think she knows what she's saying most of the time. But last night she glanced over at the other bed in her room and said, 'Look at those two sitting there on that bed, waiting for me.'"

"Were you sitting on the bed?"

"No, there was no one sitting on the bed. Then at one time she murmured, 'I may not be able to breathe right, but I'm still alive. I'm not going. They can wait all they want.' She's fighting it. I wish she wouldn't fight it so much."

"Jennifer has been a fighter all her life, Christine, and this is just a natural process of her thinking. It's not that she's fighting death so much, as it is just Jennifer."

"These past five years were the best we had as sisters. Before then, deep down in my heart I used to resent her for being more beautiful than me, more popular than me, more intelligent than me. But when I changed my attitude toward her, we discovered a closeness that I'd never known before. The other night Mother was up with her all night. She told me, 'I said to myself, Wouldn't it be great if she goes tonight?' And you know what, I was thinking the same thing."

"It must be very tough seeing her like that."

"She doesn't appear to be in pain, but when we ask her she says, Yes, she's in pain. She talks as if she's outside her body already, like 'Jennifer is having a bad day.'"

Bob called the next morning. "Jennifer died last night," he said. "Her parents said to her yesterday, 'It's all right for you to go Jennifer. It's okay to leave us.'"

There is a pattern accentuating the need for a loved one to be given permission to die. One of the more poignant cases reported in the media decades ago was that of a 3-year-old terminal boy I'll call Chuck asking his father, "Let me go Dad, let me go home." In April 1996, Baseball Hall-of-Famer Rod Carew describing the family's last moments with his 18-year-old daughter Michelle (who had fought off leukemia for seven months) said, "All we did was, we told her that we love her, that we're all here, and I just told her to have a safe journey."

Christine once mused, "I realized that the dream had been not so much to prepare me to help Jennifer, as it had been given to help me."

I believe that the brain, through dreams, not only flashes forward to the future, but links us to a past forever engraved in the universe—a central realm where everything that occurs in our universe, or that will ever occur, is recorded. Some refer to this process as tuning in to the *Akashic* or *Soul Records,* or *Book of Life,* a sphere beyond time and space. The clairvoyant, Edgar

Cayce (1877-1945) believed that all he had to do was penetrate these etheric recordings to retrieve a message. Calling himself a very simple conservative Christian man, Cayce, who had not even graduated from elementary school, in self-imposed trance would become multi-lingual, give expert medical diagnoses on people thousands of miles away and offer literate discourses on man's beginnings and destiny. When working to help others through his reading of the Akashic records, Cayce had trained himself to recall nothing on waking.

Swiss psychologist and psychiatrist Carl C. Jung (1875-1961) who believed that he tuned in to these type of available records, coined the phrase Collective Unconscious, to describe shared experiences of the human species accessible in the dream state, no matter what their culture or where they lived.

Some other scientists believe in a universal existence of individual magnetic fields, each with its own memory system. An example of this would be religious euphoria such as reported by whirling dervishes, or shamans.

In my decades of personal research, I had discerned three distinct levels of altered states of communication:

First:
At the earth level, where energies from other consciousness not in our present physical state, migrate to connect with the human species on our planet. Some would consider angels who help a person in transition at this level. Others would associate this theory with stories depicted in the mid 90s popular television series "Touched by an Angel."
Second:
At a mid-level, away from the planet earth between the physical human species consciousness and the next level of the soul. An out-of-body transformation and dream connections would be examples.

Third:
> At the highest plane of awareness, which some refer to as the level of Universal or God consciousness, or Nirvana. This entails the soul of a Homo sapiens leaving the planet earth environment and migrating to pure Spirit. Some reported experiences of global religious icons would fall in this category.

The year Mary and Mother died I learned much. But it was only the evolutionary beginning of my odyssey into the cosmos.

Chapter 7

Crossings

Jake and I were keenly aware and very grateful that our marriage was blessed with shared values and two loving, caring, healthy sons. The boys were born while Jake was still in college where, with the support of the GI Bill, he sometimes worked at three part-time jobs simultaneously—he pumped gas, he drove a cab, he sold encyclopedias door-to-door—anything to keep him in college.

After receiving his civil engineering degree, with Jake as the principal breadwinner I had the economic freedom to pursue my bottomless hunger for spiritual knowledge, and a deep need to help others which had began as a child and magnified after my flash healing at 16. Students of spiritual growth and hatha yoga, friends, and friends of friends, were drawn to me for comfort. I counseled, helped soften their dilemma, shared their tears and laughter, listened in the middle of the night.

Marc and Allen were in college when the company of which Jake was a board member dissolved. Jake accepted a position as Vice President of a leading manufacturer of strategic products used in commercial buildings, managing one of their branch factories. Soon, he was pressured into approving a family of defective batches for installation in high-rise buildings, placing structures and, of course, lives of people, at risk.

Jake was firm. No, he couldn't condone those practices. Yes he could, came instructions from the top. He could, but he wouldn't—under any circumstances. Word bubbled out that he was going to be fired and his department heads approached him with a plan to ignite a protest. No, don't do that, Jake calmly instructed his supervising staff, It will put your own jobs in jeopardy. Jake was slapped with a request for his resignation.

So what! we thought. Our security is God, and He means it for good. Besides, we had regularly done the right thing and God had always taken care of us. Marc was finishing his graduate studies, and Allen was a university senior majoring in two fields. It was going to be okay, we agreed, the timing could have been more crucial. There began a period where every door Jake knocked on slammed shut in his face. Days turned into weeks; weeks into months; and months into years. In the flicker of an eyelash we had been flushed out of Eden, and didn't know why. I accepted end-to-end temporary secretarial assignments and Jake worked at a stream of short-term jobs.

Then, after two years, the answer to our prayers: a promising career opportunity for Jake in Minneapolis. We moved with soaring expectations. There, only a few months after Mother's death, saddled with labor's refusal to accept management's new direction structured by Jake, his position was eliminated. That same week, Greg was diagnosed with Hepatitis B contracted from a blood transfusion. It was like being hurled against a brick wall with no footholds. In my journal I wrote:

> What happened to our peaceful, joyful, happy lives? First God took my home away, then Jake's job, then my sister, then my mother. Now Greg's in the hospital, Jake's dignity shaky. Everything negative that had eluded our family now appears to be making up for our happy years. I cannot conceive of any father, let alone a loving God Father/Mother, leaving us to be tossed in turbulent waters in a storm.

One evening, very much sensing Mary's presence, I wrote on my pad:

"Mary, have you been there long enough to know why man suffers here? Why are we going through this?"

Chapter 7

> *"We all go through whatever we need to learn from our experiences. You are growing closer to truth and need to pass certain tests and temptations when it appears that all is falling apart. But God's love is always with you."*

When in my teens we lived in Eritrea (a former Italian colony), I was dubbed La Primavera (Springtime) because they said my happy nature was as welcome as spring, always there to share the joy of being alive in a universe with a God as "all things good." So the justifications I got in my writings from Mary—tests and temptations in a world that appeared to be coming apart—carried an alien weight.

"What about your turmoil and suffering here on earth, Mary?" I asked.

"I learned from my suffering. I am happy and busy working with new souls who come here."

"You're talking about redemptive love like yours. What about Jennifer's suffering. She didn't want to die. She didn't want to suffer."

"We are helping Jennifer to adjust. Her soul will be with us for a while. She wants to return to earth and have her physical body again. She needs to learn some things here and then she'll return. We will all be given the opportunity to learn and grow closer to Truth."

Minnesota had recently passed a law allowing doctors to declare a person physically dead when all brain activity ceased. I'd been thinking a great deal about Mary's disclosure of having left her body before she was officially declared dead. I called the hospital in San Francisco, and was put through to the supervising nurse on the surgery floor. "I remember Mary well," she said. "We were all so very fond of her."

"I would simply like to find out if her records show that Mary's heart had ever stopped and been resuscitated," I said. "And if her brain activity had ceased before her expiration."

"Give me a minute" she answered. "I've got to retrieve her chart."

When she returned she explained: "It shows here that there were two episodes of Code Blue." She hesitated. "You really need to contact her physician, Dr. Brown. I'll give you her telephone number."

At Dr. Brown's office I was told she couldn't be reached. I requested that she call me collect. After waiting for several weeks, I sent a letter with a self-addressed, stamped envelope asking specifically if Mary had been brain dead before her heart stopped. I never heard from Dr. Brown.

Just before the first anniversary of Mary's transition, one night, after thrashing and tossing because of Jake's snoring, I had opted for the hide-a-bed in the den when suddenly I sensed that someone had entered my room. With my heart pounding like a grandfather clock, I opened my eyes and discovered a frozen silhouette at the window with its back to me.

Oh my God, who's that? Here I am, all alone in this room. What's this thing going to do to me, for Jake's such a heavy sleeper he won't even hear what's going on. I watched. The figure stood very still, gazing out at the shimmering swimming pool compound. The serene aura was like soothing salve, and I reared up to study the persona. It was an outline of a woman.

Silver moonlight bounced in from around the form, and a bluish light seeped from the large picture windows in the adjacent living room. In that Antarctic hush, as I concentrated on the figure at the window, it pirouetted facing the interior of the room. Now unafraid, I focused all of my energies to determine who it was. With head and body poised like royalty carrying a heavy crown, the form began striding toward me and stopped at the foot of my bed. Then I knew. It was either Mother, or Mary. But how? They're both dead.

As if sailing on ice, the person moved to my side. And I recognized my sister, a loving magical smile on her beaming face.

Galvanized, I gape. Am I too dead? Am I still breathing? Caught in the marvel of our reunion my fears evaporate, and, like old times when we'd sit up in bed together and talk for hours, I scoot over, turn down the coverings on her side and say, "Get in." In fluid rhythm, Mary unwraps some sort of cloudy outer mantle and smoothly slides in under the blanket.

Although I clearly see her head resting on the pillow I want to take a closer look, so rearing up on an elbow I gawk, "It *is* you, isn't it?" She simply smiles. Stunned, I shift closer to validate this miracle. She looks as she did when 19, with translucent skin and rosy cheeks; happy and healthy and vibrant. "Do you know you look beautiful?" I say. And so peaceful, I think.

Still smiling, telepathically she says, "You don't. You don't look good." Well naturally I don't look as good as she does, I think, she's much younger than I am.

As if I've spoken out loud, Mary shakes her head and softly says, "No, you are not well." I know she's referring to my health. Then she adds, "You're going to get better."

She lies serenely. I continue to stare.

From the next bedroom I hear Jake's voice, "I'm coming over, and I'm not decent."

"I've got to leave," Mary announces. Climbing out of bed, she shakes out a wispy emerald color scarf-like sheath which shimmers like muted rays of sunshine. I know she has a long journey ahead. And I know I can't stop her.

She glides away, becoming fainter and fainter. And vaporizes.

My eyes were open, but I was saturated in a cosmic throb. When I knew the energy in my physical body was alive, I looked at the clock. It was exactly midnight. I listened for sounds in the next bedroom. Nothing. I slipped back into sleep. At dawn I rose and woke up Jake.

"What are you doing up so early?" he mumbled.

"Do you remember anything unusual about last night?"

He sat up. "Unusual? No. You must have left and gone to the other room to sleep. That's not unusual."

"Any dreams? Do you remember any dreams at all?"

"Sweetheart, I know everyone is supposed to dream, but I never remember my dreams. You know that. Why?"

. "Mary came to me last night," I said.

"She did."

"And you wouldn't believe how great she looked."

"I believe it," Jake said calmly.

I told him all the details, and his announcement that he was going to join us. "Are you sure you don't remember anything at all?" I prodded.

"Lisa, you've told me how most people don't remember these types of communication."

"Your voice was so clear, I thought you were awake."

"No, not me. One psychic in the family's enough, Sweetheart," he smiled.

I'd been feeling lousy and that morning I was scheduled to go in for some blood work. A few days later, I got a call from the Clinic telling me that all test results were normal.

Anxious to get some answers in writing, I asked:

Chapter 7

"Mary, was it hard for you to show yourself to me? Did it take a lot of energy?"

"Yes. I am always with you. But I have to do a lot of work for you to see me. And you have to be aware."

"I've been hoping that I can come there. Wouldn't that be easier for you?"

"You do come here but you don't remember."

In my journal I wrote:

> I know that Mother and Mary's consciousness is continuing on a level which is not visible to me. And, now that it is over a year since Mary's death, my search for answers is not so much because I miss them (although to my surprise I feel their loss at the most unexpected times), but it is this insatiable curiosity that constantly agitates my impatient need to understand the universe.

> There has to be a reason for existence. No matter how hard I have tried, I cannot accept as truth that man exists and expands in his knowledge and consciousness and then, through what we call death, suddenly everything is turned off; completely and irreversibly gone. If there's an argument that everything in the universe goes through the process of birth, maturity and death, then what happens to those who die at a physically young age?

That summer of 1979 launched the most crucial cosmic appointment in my spiritual search. A soul-to-soul missile heralded the dawn of a union's transition; a rendezvous that affirmed the timeless, spaceless reaches of universal consciousness.

Chapter 8

The Soul's Embrace

Carved into the kaleidoscope of life are births and graduations and weddings and first-time milestones and last-time goodbyes, and sometimes the unpredictable and unexplainable. Memorial Day weekend 1979, started out as a miracle of springtime in just-getting-over a bone-chilling Minneapolis winter, and concluded as the most pulse-stopping apex of cosmic consciousness chiseled into my psyche.

Following our apartment complex annual picnic, we stretched out indoors relaxing in the evening glow of a three-day holiday. Later, as cool breezes swirled through our open windows and the moon was ivory in the velvet skies, we lay side-by-side on the sofa watching a made-for-television movie, *The Best Place To Be,* starring Donna Reed as Sheila. The tale revolved around the recovery of the protagonist from the death of her philandering husband, Sean, who expires from a first-time heart attack on his way home from a secret tryst.

After the movie followed by the news we headed for bed, but the portrait of a wife who's confronted with the sudden loss of her spouse chilled me, and I kept hammering at Jake about the agonizing shock of a fatal first heart attack. "Why am I so bothered by it?" I wondered. "Perhaps because there was no warning, no mental preparation. Nothing."

"Sweetheart, these are just stories," Jake stressed. "It doesn't happen that often."

He was right. Life was on a promising path of balance again. Jake was into setting up his own construction business, and prospects looked good. Sure, we were still in an apartment, but

Chapter 8

the possibility of nesting in our own home twinkled like the first evening star. Our boys, the Northern Lights of our life now with cum laude degrees, were tasting life as independent wage-earning men; Marc in Chicago, Allen in Northern California. And we got together for birthdays, vacations, holidays and times in between. I fell asleep grateful for blessings.

At the cusp of midnight, a pulsing stillness like the white echoes of Alaska's mountains spurred me awake demanding my attention. And a universal communication signaled that a special someone was patiently waiting to be recognized. Separated by an ocean of sunset-pinks and moonlight silvers like tiers of clouds one soars through in a jet plane, an entity energized into focus blinking, "Pay attention. Identify who I am."

Standing very still, where the cosmos embrace the horizon, I was startled to recognize Jake posed exactly as he did waiting for me at the altar. But not the Jake who never missed flashing me a smile. This one was serious, and penetrating, with a tinge of sadness. He rose at my left, eons away yet telepathically intimate, and though not understanding how or why I was aware that the unblinking panorama that parted us couldn't be bridged. My immediate reaction was, Why isn't he smiling? This was not simply Jake's physical incarnation. It was the genuine entity—Jake's pure soul. Gratified that I grasped it was he, Jake stressed, "Lisa, you must remember."

"I will."

"Absolutely. You must," he pressed.

"I'll remember," I pledged.

In a telepathic, calculated instructional cadence much like a teacher's dialog with a student, Jake said, "I'm going to be with you only one-and-half years."

What? What does that mean? His piercing blue eyes imprisoned me in a hypnotic bond. Only one-and-half years with me? What is one-and-half years? Why isn't he saying eighteen months? It would be more precise. Does it mean he's not going to be around after that? Where's he going to be?

In the unceasing telepathic tempo this entity, this Jake's soul, persisted, "You must remember." Of course I'll remember, I agreed.

The scenario dissipated.

Partially awake but oblivious of my physical environment, I directed my subconscious to retain the ethereal eruption. Then, certain that it was now indelibly scripted in my brain cells, fell asleep.

In the morning, for the merest instant, I reasoned I must have imagined my spiritual rendezvous. But every component of my encounter flashed back in vivid sequence, and my pledge to remember blazed like the promise of the American flag as I repeated the citizenship oath. Had I been jostled into a journey of the Akashic records? I had no other explanation.

Jake had always prided himself on his good health, and my mantra to him was, "You come from a line of long-lived people." Women on his mother's side lived into their 90s and 100s, men on both sides at least into their 60s. At the end of the year-and-half Jake would just be turning 52.

When Jake bounced out of bed in his customary let's-get-this-day-on-the-road zest, I watched for signs of preoccupation. There were none. At our leisurely holiday breakfast, I ventured, "Did you sleep well?"

Rolling his head back, taking a deep breath he announced, "Fantastic. You know me, once I fall asleep that's it. Did you?"

"Yeah."

"Why are you saying it like that?"

"Like what?"

"Y-e-a-h! Like that. You don't sound right."

"I don't?"

"No. Did you have a dream?"

Chapter 8

I needed time to sort things out. "I had something. . . . Maybe it was that movie last night."

"Why? You think *I* could be having an illicit, secret affair?"

Gazing deep into those oceanic eyes I teased, "Are you?"

"Well-l-l, . . . now that you've brought it up . . ."

Jake was in such good spirits, I wished the odyssey was an illusion. "I didn't bring it up, you did," I grinned, sticking my chin up in the air.

Pushing his chair back, he pranced to my side. "In that case, no," he murmured as he gathered my hand, one finger at a time, lifting it up turned it over and lingeringly, soothingly pressed his warm lips to the center of my palm. "You know you're my only girl," he added reaching down and drawing me up against him, "But, you'd better be good to me."

"I'm always good to you."

"Just remember that," he whispered in my ear.

All is well, I thought. If I refuse to believe in it, perhaps it'll not happen. But I knew I had to confront the oracle some time, for I'd pledged my word. What could I do about it? What was I supposed to do about it?

Many years earlier, when our sons were 12 and 10, there was another forewarning. It was a symbolic message, not a direct missile like this one. It saved my life.

It was the autumn of 1965. We were living in a Chicago suburb. That week, heavy rains and storms had flooded basements, toppled trees and caused numerous disasters initiating evacuations in our county. Fortunately, it had skipped our immediate neighborhood.

1965 was the year Christian churches were in a concerted ecumenical movement, stressing similarities, togetherness and collaboration. At the 1964-1965 World Fair in New York City, a half-hour movie entitled *The Parable,* sponsored by the Protestant & Orthodox Center, had stirred mountains of controversy because it presented Christ as a mime in a circus setting. In an effort to promote unity of Christian denominations, the Organization of Churches arranged structured community forums, targeting the thesis of the movie for discussion.

In my town, a Sunday evening forum was scheduled at the Roman Catholic cathedral, to be monitored by pre-designated persons from participating churches. Following a showing of *The Parable,* the congregation was to break up into small discussion groups of ten. We expected a gathering of 400-500, and I was one of the assigned discussion leaders.

On the morning of the forum, I awakened before dawn not quite sure where I was. I opened my eyes with difficulty, and concentrated on my physical surroundings. In the dim twilight I eventually picked out familiar objects in our bedroom, and knew I was safe at home in bed. But something was different.

Although my brain signaled parts of my body to move, I had no motor ability: the leg I tried to stretch wouldn't shift; an arm resting by my head just lay there as if dismembered. I wanted to pull the blanket tighter around my cold neck, but it stayed loosely draped around my chilled, rigid body. I felt as if I were just coming out from very heavy sedation into a nonconforming reality, suspended weightless in space between two opposing energies—the material world where my body lay, and the more urgent pulsating one in my consciousness.

An electrical silence dominated everywhere.

I became drowsy. Struggling to stay awake, my mind gradually focused on a crucial scenario. A dream. Vibrations in my head, mingling with a monotonous whistling in my ears evolved into a sixth dimension. And the dream restarted like a movie on a screen.

In the evening of a cloudy day, after some heavy rains, the skies had cleared and the roads were safely dry. I was driving north on a very familiar four-lane divided superhighway near our home, and approached a spot where traffic always whizzed by uneventfully. The landmarks were very pronounced: a service station on the left, a vacant field of tall dry autumn grass sheltering an old farm on the right, and a major intersection a mile ahead.

With no previous warning my car hesitated, and I realized that the road was flooded. The waters appeared unthreateningly shallow, so to drive through swiftly I pressed harder on the accelerator. But instead of picking up speed, my vehicle slowed down, the engine died, and I felt the tires leave solid ground as, trapped in a major flood, the car sunk deeper and deeper in turbid waters. Weightless, my body rose with my hair twirling in a sinuous dance around my face. Hold on to the steering wheel, don't let go, were my explicit instructions from somewhere. I clung to the steering wheel.

Round and round and round the car swirled in a hypnotic clockwise rhythm, sinking lower and lower into a bottomless muddy whirlpool of death. But I wouldn't let go. Determined, I clasped the steering wheel tighter.

The slashing sounds of the waters blended with the vibrations in my head and synthesized with the ringing in my ears soaring into an ominous melody of doom. It was like watching myself die in slow motion on a life-size movie screen.

I knew it was a dream, but in straining to escape to the physical world of reality the portentous melody gripped me, insisting that I acknowledge its theme. It was horrible. I was very scared. Not of dying so much, as scared of the depth of that whirlpool. (I've always had a neurotic fear of water that has prevented me from learning to swim.)

To loosen the paralyzing power of the dream, after several unsuccessful attempts I managed to get up. Jake was sleeping. I eased into our sons' bedroom. Both were also sound asleep. I had to keep physically active, for if I stopped the haunting vibrations pursued me sarcastically. Holding on to the railing for balance, I traipsed downstairs to the kitchen and reached for the coffee maker. Daylight was just beginning to break.

The significance of the dream was very clear: danger; death. With no prior warning, there will appear in my life a fatally treacherous hazard, which will marshal me into a violent demise.

Yet, what can any person do with the confrontation of impending death? One thing I recognized: such knowledge immediately sharpens an appreciation of life and all its joys.

As I waited for the family to wake up, I decided to postpone telling them about my dream until I could explicitly resolve what I should do. The next day, I'd be alone and have time to reflect on possible practical answers.

That bright, brisk Sunday, we enjoyed a family barbecue and some vigorous badminton in our back yard.

Once Jake said to me, "Do you feel well?"

"I'm fine."

"No, you're not."

"I had a dream which I'm trying to figure out," I mused.

"Is it bad?"

"Oh, I don't think so," I hedged.

"Will you tell me when you know?"

Not to alarm him, I said "Sure."

As the day progressed, the mesmerizing melody in my head returned with less frequency and by evening I'd managed to put aside my trauma. When it was time for me to leave for the ecumenical meeting, Jake suggested that I take our recently acquired Mercury sedan.

"No," I shrugged, "that's your car. My old Ford is fine."

"Lisa, you'll be returning home late at night. The Mercury will not give you any problems. Take it," he insisted.

So, at dusk, I rolled onto the four-lane divided highway at the wheel of our gleaming new auto musing about how much shorter the days were becoming and how much sooner we were

Chapter 8

turning on our lights. The evening was clear, the air calm, the traffic was light and my vehicle purred like a domesticated tiger. I had completely forgotten my dream.

A mile from home, heading north to the town center, I was in the left lane with two cars on my right On the other side of the divided highway, the southbound lanes were empty. Casually, I noticed headlights in the horizon appearing to travel at a very high speed, and as the beams got brighter I started to get uneasy.

Suddenly, like a laser ignition, I recognized my locale: the landmark in my dream—service station on the west, vacant land with the little farm tucked away in the background on the east.

The rhythmic whir of tires on the blacktop triggered the monotonous sinking strains of that whirlpool in my head, and the peaceful country night transformed into a symbol of death. O my God, the flood! That instantaneous trap in my dream.

I knew there was a car careening south, not on the other side of the divided highway, but in the wrong northbound lane. And I was directly in its path.

My first reaction was to pull off to the shoulder. But there was no shoulder—only a low grass median, too soaked from the recent storms to support my car. My next reaction was to press down hard on the horn. That wouldn't do—it would panic the other two drivers on my right and we'd all pile up on top of each other. What if I came to a complete stop in my lane? Of course, I'd be hit. Should I try to pass the first car on my right? No time. This is how I'm going to die—in a head-on collision. Our car with less than 500 miles will be totaled. What a waste! I wish I were driving my faithful standby. And my family? How will Jake manage? How will the boys grow up without a mother?

Then a voice signaled: The steering wheel, hang on to the steering wheel. Just as in your dream, hang on. Don't give up. I switched my turn signal on, took my foot off the gas and searched for space at my right. Abruptly, the first car picked up speed. Pumping my brakes, almost blinded by the glare now bearing down upon me, I inched between the two cars just as the southbound auto rumbled by like a ferocious earthquake.

Lights, brakes, squealing tires, noise, wind, all melded into a thunderous tremor. The car ahead rushed on. And, because I didn't know what else to do, I kept going. Had I been hit? My teeth chattered, my foot on the accelerator trembled violently, and I had trouble staying in my lane. Please, please God, I prayed, just let me get to the cathedral.

I arrived, not sure whether my wobbly knees would hold me up. Easing out of my seat, I slowly orbited the car looking for damages especially checking and rechecking the left rear end, but the metal felt smooth under my quivering fingers. How did I escape that monster from nowhere?

Inside, the movie had just ended and the discussion circles were being formed. I played my role of group leader, but a part of me still felt trapped on the highway. When I spoke my voice sounded strange and echoed in my head, and often I had to bite my tongue to prevent my teeth from chattering.

I remember a bell indicating the end of the meeting, but I don't remember getting in my car, or driving home, or parking the auto in the garage. I remember turning off the lights that Jake had left on for me and crawling in bed completely exhausted, mentally repeating over and over, "Thank you, God."

The next day I jotted down the episode and put it away. In the evening, after Marc and Allen were in bed, I told Jake what had happened. "I knew something was wrong yesterday," he said, "even though you kept insisting No."

"That dream was so cryptic," I explained, "I needed to straighten it out in my own mind first. Telling it to you as it was would only have worried you."

Years later, when I began a correspondence with Dr. Karlis Osis, Director, The American Society for Psychical Research,

Inc., he requested verification of the incident from Jake, who in part wrote:

> Lisa's frequent and accurate predictions are so routine in our home that we accept them, and forget them, as with the daily newspaper. Of the experience she reported to you, I recall only the barest of essentials. . . . Lisa did have a rather disturbing dream. . . . When she told me later of her narrow escape from a traffic accident involving a car approaching her on the wrong side of a divided highway, I was not surprised.

Jake proceeded to tell Dr. Osis of a dream predicting a series of personal events for him which he'd originally dismissed as unlikely, but occurred exactly as I'd foreseen.

Most parapsychologists agree that, for those with deep intimate ties, mental telepathy, whether asleep or awake, is a very common medium of communication, especially, at times of sorrow or joy.

Henry, a business acquaintance, once discussed with me an experience he had in the Navy during the Vietnam war. One night he had decided to stay on board while Norm, his closest friend and cabin-mate, went out on the town. "I woke up at four in the morning with the feeling that something was wrong," Henry described. "I wasn't sure what. Just that something was grave, and I had to do something about it. Norm was not in his bunk. Typically, I would have gone back to sleep, but I felt that he needed me. I got up, dressed, and went out to the pier. It was black, I couldn't see anything, and everything seemed quiet. I kept going over to a certain spot at the end of a plank, walking away, then going back to the spot again as if pulled by a magnet. Not finding anything, I had no choice but to return. But I couldn't sleep. Again, I got up, dressed and this time went and told my superior officer that Norm was not in his bunk.

"While we were talking, a commotion started. A body had been sighted overboard. All hands were called, and the person was pulled out. It was Norm. He was unconscious, but had been floating with his head above water. He survived. Later Norm told me that the last thing he remembered was calling my name."

In researching precognitive incidents, I had learned that Dr. Ian Stevenson (at the time with the University of Virginia), had found strong evidence that precognitive or clairvoyant communications of death, or disaster, are received very close to the actual incidents predicted. This supported my own experiences in cosmic experiences.

So, what was the one-and-half year span?

Jake loved deeply, unconditionally and selflessly, with an endearing quality of being protective without a suffocating possessiveness. Recognizing my need for independence, he allowed me freedom to pursue my goals and formulate conclusions with no restraints. Jake's parents were divorced when he was 5, precipitating a painful shuttle between residences at a time when a low percent of marriages ended in divorce. At 15 he had left home, working nights and going to school days. Because our backgrounds were so dissimilar, our bond of over thirty years challenged predictions that our marriage would be short-lived, and I'd say to him often, "Jake, I get bored with everything except with you."

Because Jake had married a non-U.S. citizen, immediately after our wedding his top security clearance was revoked, and we were flown to his home in Indiana on temporary leave to await reassignment. One afternoon Jake led me into a small neighborhood grocery store to introduce his new bride to his decades older pal, Joe Meyer. After barely touching my hand in a limp-lettuce shake, in an aside Joe demanded, "What's the matter kid? Aren't there American girls here good enough for you?" I wished the floor would slash open and shoot me back to Africa. As if revealing a long-hidden family secret to a younger sibling, Jake put an arm across Joe's bony hunched shoulder and said, "You see Joe, it's like this. Some go for quantity. I go for quality."

After that Memorial Day rendezvous, whenever I struggled to flush away the psychic missile my solemn promise to remember would zap my soul like a tornado. I watched for clues that Jake recognized our limited time together. There were none. Should I tell the boys? I elected not to say anything until compelled to do so, for concealing it made the tremor less threatening. Besides, Jake, as usual, was in excellent health.

I took an ordinary, 8½×11 ruled paper loose-leaf tablet, the ones that have a red line for the margin, and hastily scribbled:

Memorial Day, May 28, '79.

> Last night I had an experience: In the middle of the night I 'dreamt' that Jake appeared and said: "I have only 1½ years with you." (Then, afraid to highlight the terror of such a prediction added), I don't know whether this was because I watched a movie with Donna Reed about a woman whose husband dies suddenly of a heart attack. Or it could be a temptation for me to believe in a negative experience.

I tore the sheet off and stowed it away with my journals. Deep in the recesses of our filing cabinet. Somewhere, where Jake would not stumble on it.

Chapter 9

Unto the Fold

Jake was successful in acquiring a steel buildings franchise, and began setting up a construction business in accordance with Minnesota laws. My job as an executive secretary provided essential health insurance benefits. In the fall, with the approach of the slow winter construction season in that icy state abutting Canada, Allen prodded his father into looking at alternative careers in Northern California, specifically the video industry, then in its infancy.

Although Jake was a civil engineering and construction buff, he flew to the West Coast to research video retail franchises, where, following a week in Los Angeles, he and Allen began to scan prospective Silicon Valley store locations. Jake now faced a major career change decision which entailed abandoning his chosen field where he'd not only been respected as a proficient, caring, team-playing boss, but one which had earned him a place in *Who's Who in the Midwest* for the last four years.

With Jake away, late one night I picked up the phone and dialed Marc in Chicago. It was time for me to share the secret I had masked in the caravan of my denials.

"Mom, I was just thinking about you," Marc said. "Are you all right? Is Dad still in San Francisco?"

"Yes he is," I answered, ignoring the first question. "While Dad's away, I wanted to talk with you."

"I was going to call you, but thought this would be late. You're usually asleep by now."

"Yeah, I usually am. I've been thinking a great deal about a dream I had some time ago."

"You have?"

"It was more . . . more like an altered state of consciousness. A cosmic connection."

"It was?" I didn't have to explain any more, for the boys had grown up taking my psychic premonitions for granted.

"Marc, your father's soul came to me one night and told me that he was going to be with me only for one-and-half years."

"His soul?"

"Yes, his soul. His real self. He was asleep. And, he's not aware it happened."

"When was this?"

"Memorial weekend."

"Six months ago? Mom, are you sure?"

"Marc, I'm sure. It was your father."

"It was!"

"The time-frame shook me. Even during the dream I kept thinking, Why doesn't he say eighteen months, it would be more precise. But I think it's significant."

The ticktock of my clock on the wall boomed like Big Ben.

Jake's sons were the apex of his soul. Because I'd grown up without the harboring presence of a father, I marveled at the exhilarating bond of fatherhood which nurtured Jake's essence and navigated the boys over the rocky bumps of coming-of-age. Now, confiding my secret to Marc underlined my denials.

Marc said "Mom, tell me again exactly what it was." I went over the details carefully.

"Well," Marc sighed. "If Dad has only one year left, I want him to do what he likes best. He's always been happy in the construction business. I don't want him starting all over with something new." I agreed. What to do! I'd always given Jake complete freedom to make his own decisions about career moves.

The next morning, Allen called to say his dad was on the flight home. "He's decided not to go into the video business," he added.

"You sound disappointed."

"Yes, I am. Very."

Trying to keep it low key, cautiously I outlined my soul-to-soul missile to Allen. Irate, he demanded, "What percentage of these dreams come true?"

Though I was 98 percent sure of the authenticity of the cosmic touch, to appease the shock I said, "For dreams, generally, about eighty-five. In this case, I'll be conservative and say ninety percent."

"Well Mom," Allen declared, "this is going to be that other ten."

Jake continued the expansion of his business. For Memorial Day weekend 1980, Allen flew us to Northern California where he and Trish announced their engagement, with plans to get married in October.

"Dad, you've got to move here," Allen urged his father again. "If you want to stay in construction, why not do it here? The Silicon Valley is bursting with all kinds of growing businesses propelled by the computer industry. I know sooner or later, you'll find exactly what you'll want here."

Jake wasn't ready for a major change. His steel building franchise connections were progressing well.

As our wedding anniversary in August approached, I wanted to present Jake a gift which could come only from me. Throughout the years, in addition to special occasion cards, we had both saved letters penned to each other. This year, though we were not going to be apart, I decided to put down in writing and give to him as my anniversary gift, my appreciation of his love and caring.

This was a decision that, for the rest of my life, spotlighted the significance of not only appreciating each day for its joys, but also the value of making sure loved ones are unconditionally, intimately aware how cherished and special they are.

Tucked inside an anniversary card, my letter in part said:

Tomorrow is our 29th wedding anniversary and I find myself reflecting and re-appraising our lives together trying to realistically list the debits and credits, the trials and rewards, the successes and failures. Although we have had our share of disappointments, our lives together have still been filled with an overwhelming amount of blessings. Among the 'good things' has always been, and will always be, you in my life. I thank you for asking me to share your life, and if your love should end today, I am still very blessed for having your calm influence, your love and devotion to me and the boys all these years.

These past four years have not been very easy for you, but I want you to know that the boys and I love you enough to allow you to work things out your own way. Our faith and trust in you will always remain unshakable.

Our love for each other and the beautiful relationship we share with our sons being the two top priorities in my life, I would pronounce my life completely fulfilled, if ever everything else fell apart. You have worked very hard to make us happy, perhaps it is now our turn to work a little to make you happy.

The next morning, with a tender kiss, Jake handed me his reply. In part it read:

With you around, life has no disappointments—only a few variations. This is probably what true love is. Not the perpetual excitement of good entertainment, but a calm constant glow of love, warmth, sharing, and the pleasure of giving happiness. You have done all of these things for me and nothing else is really important to me except my family. And my greatest pleasure and comfort is making you happy. For nearly thirty years not only have I had the things I really wanted, but the best.

Professionally, I am satisfied, too. With your support, and trusting in God, I was unafraid to accept challenge, and have accomplished more than I ever thought possible.

All I want is to continue contributing, enjoy productivity, and have financial independence. I am grateful for good health, but I want to provide you the economic freedom to spend your time writing.

Because of you, the love in our family, together with the happiness we have shared, I feel totally fulfilled. But should I not make it, it's all right, for I've received in thirty years what some cannot get in a hundred lifetimes.

His letter has remained my most cherished gem.

At the beginning of fall, a dream, repeating over and over like a rewound movie, shook me awake every time I fell asleep. On a clear, bright day, around noon I'm driving up a hill, carefree and secure in the privacy of my car. After the climb to the summit, with no other vehicles on the road, I start to make a right turn when, with no warning, my car stops dead. Suddenly, the bright, sunny day is gone and there is a blizzard. Although the windows are closed, and the car sealed tight, snow crystals begin to float inside. I hear the wind howling, whoosh, whoosh, whoosh. I've got to get away and out of here. I try to start the car. Nothing! My former safe haven is buried in an asphyxiating snowdrift.

That solitary, trapped and abandoned feeling plagued me. I decided not to share the dream with Jake, and our cosmic soul contact haunted me more and more. In Minneapolis Jake and I were alone, away from Marc and Allen, away from my brothers and nurturing relatives, and away from long-time friends we had left behind. Jake was healthy, but what if, for some unknown reason, he does die? How would I cope all alone?

As we made plans to attend Allen and Trish's wedding in October, Jake accelerated the completion of his outdoor jobs before the onslaught of snows, and the foreboding *Akashic* missile haunted me like a rushing river crumbling its sandy banks.

One evening after dinner, I was spread out on the sofa waiting for Jake to finish working on his books.

"Nothing good on TV tonight?" he questioned as he crawled in behind me.

"I haven't checked yet."

Chapter 9

With his tingling fingers stroking wisps of hair behind my ear, he purred "Hmm, maybe better things ahead."

I scrambled around. "Jake, I've been thinking."

"O-h h-o, that could be dangerous."

"No, really. I've been thinking that if something should ever happen to either one of us, the other would be left all alone out here." Those sparkling blue oceans, took on a hint of a cloud. "Now that the boys are settled, I wonder whether it wouldn't be wise for us to just pick up and move to be nearer one of them."

"Lisa, why pick up now when I've gotten started in my business?"

"Sweetheart, you've always wanted to live in warmer weather. Maybe this is the time to move to California. We'd be near Allen, and we'd live in a beautiful climate."

He sat up and reached for a cigarette. "Yes, it's true that I don't like cold weather," he agreed. "Allen says opportunities are booming in Silicon Valley, but I'm beginning to make the right contacts here. The bank is behind me, the farmers need buildings. I'm visible in the business community. We'd be taking a huge risk to just pick up and move. We'll both have to start all over again."

He made sense.

November, the pivotal one-and-half year was zooming in. Jake was going to turn 52 on the first. Was it going to be his last year?

I thought of his 23rd birthday. It was the first winter we were in the States, and the day he introduced his new wife from Africa to snow. We were staying with his parents in Indianapolis waiting for reassignment from Eritrea. That morning when I opened my eyes Jake was already dressed. "Wait a minute," he said, "don't get up," and rushing outside returned with his cupped hands overflowing with a fine, powdery white substance. "See?" he stretched his palms, "this is snow. Want to feel it?"

I glanced outside at a world sheeted in silver, then reached over to let the white, cold powder chill through my fingers. Like a 4-year-old who has just sailed downhill in her first snow wagon, I giggled, "Wow, that's cold. You know what? It looks just like sand after a *haboob*."

"What's a 'haboob?'"

"A sandstorm. The ones we get in Sudan, only it's white. And ccold."

"Got-ya," Jake chuckled, slurping the sparkling bluish crystals against my face. In scooting away, I tumbled off the bed and he leaped on top of me as giddy with my new discovery we rolled together.

That week his orders came through: reassignment to Anchorage, Alaska.

About ten days after I had approached the subject of relocation, Jake recounted a dream he had had which, to me, was ominous. I made up some excuse to him that sometimes our fears can be so strong they become reflected in a dream, and although I knew that Jake didn't thoroughly believe my explanations, he didn't press me. And, to preserve my own sanity, I dismissed his dream from my consciousness so meticulously that I've never been able to recall the details.

Soon, a notice arrived reminding us that our apartment lease would expire at the end of November. Renewing it would mean a whole year's commitment which I knew we shouldn't do. The firm I worked for had a branch in Silicon Valley. One chilly Saturday during lunch, I eased into the subject. "Perhaps I could look into a transfer to San Jose, Jake. This way I'd be working while you get settled."

Boring deep into my eyes like the sweep of a searchlight, he said, "You've never before pursued a move this way."

"Don't you think if we're ever going to live in a better climate, now's the time?"

"Yes and no," he mused, leaning forward to rest his chin on fingers cupped in a pyramid. I knew, he knew, it wasn't only the climate.

"Jake, we've only been here two years," I reminded him. "Our close friends are all somewhere else. In addition to the climate, we'd be near Allen and Trish, and of course my brothers and Val and family."

He sighed deeply, lifted his head back and gazed at me with narrowed eyes. "You've never before wanted a move to be near relatives," he said gently.

"Yeah, I'm full of surprises aren't I?" I shot him a flirty smile. "Makes life more interesting for you Sweetheart."

He looked away then wordlessly punctured my shallow armor, and my heart started to flutter like the wings of a hummingbird as I silently repeated, I love you, that's all I want you to know.

"Hmm," he said with a faint smile. "You want to be near Allen and the relatives."

"Wouldn't that be nice, Sweetheart?"

"All right, we'll do it." he whispered.

"We will?"

"Yes."

"When?"

"We won't renew our lease. I can move us before the end of November."

"Jake, that's a long way to move ourselves." We'd never done that. The companies he worked for had always packed and moved us. "We've each got a car. And there's your pickup and equipment."

"I'll do it. It'll take two trips, but I'll do it."

We flew into action. My boss arranged a job interview for me at our Silicon Valley office. When we attended Allen and Trish's October wedding, I was offered an immediate transfer, and on December 1, Jake and I moved into an apartment less than a dozen zigzag miles from Allen and Trish. And, for the first time since our marriage, we lived within commuting distance to my own family.

We ushered 1981 with revitalized dreams. "A new beginning," I recorded in my journal. "The past is behind us. Life is good."

When networking for a position with established firms didn't pan out, Jake transferred his steel buildings franchise, prepared for the state construction contractors' licensing exam, and took over the role of keeping house. He joined a flying club and explored California from his most loved vantage point—the endless skies. He talked about joining the nearby health club where he was fast making a name as a formidable racquetball competitor.

By August, we were true Californians: we'd rumbled in two earthquakes, and Allen and Trish had watched their love-nest (purchased barely a week before their wedding), inch down the mountain in a rainstorm. The good news: Jake had gotten on the approved contractors' list of a nearby military base.

Although deep in my consciousness I could not deny that the Memorial Day weekend cosmic dialogue was an astral flash, Jake's utter oblivion made it easier for me to suppress my concerns. Allen must be right, I reasoned, that warning must have fallen in the percentage that doesn't transpire.

I convinced myself that perhaps, in the long run, it was a cosmic quake that simply vaulted our relocation.

But, was it?

Chapter 10

From This Day

For the first time since our sons had left home we lived near one of them, and having others in my family within a short freeway drive was a stabilizing sensation. August zoomed as the beginning of happy times, for Rich and Val had married only days following our wedding. "We're celebrating in style," Val announced. "Do you know how long we've waited for this? Thirty years."

Acting as our official tour guides, they picked us up Sunday morning for an all-day Mardigras. We breakfasted at the Marina in Monterey with sea gulls swooping their welcome in the azure skies dotted with see-through clouds. We lunched in Carmel with the Pacific waves whooshing and swooshing their seductive swirls. For dinner, we toasted each other at a hideaway where the candle-flames flickered to the ceiling, the music spelled romance, and the chocolate dessert was dynamite.

The next day Val and I struggled with classic hangovers. Our husbands laughed. Val kept saying, It was worth it. I kept thinking, Is this what California wine does to someone's head?

On Tuesday, our anniversary, I came home from work to a knockout fairy-tale setting. By the fireplace, long-stemmed rosebuds the color of ripe peaches spired from showers of snowflake baby-breaths. In our bedroom a tall crystal vase on the night stand flashed with thirty scarlet roses. The dining table was set for a candlelight dinner, its centerpiece a bowl of pineapple-hued miniature roses peeking from a bed of emerald leaves. And when I pulled my chair out, a card nested on a gigantic box of my favorite chocolates.

Hhhhhhh, I sniffed. "I love the fragrance of roses. Sweetheart, you certainly know how to make a wife feel special."

"You *are* special," Jake said. "Very special." Leaning over I clung to him in a lecherous kiss. "That was worth thirty years of slavery," he cooed.

Two days later I picked up the phone at 1:01 to hear a stranger say Jake was in the Emergency Room.

I dialed Allen's office. His secretary said he was at an all-day off-site meeting in Oakland. "Flo, this is Allen's mother," I said. "May I please leave a message for him?"

"Certainly, Mrs. Saddler."

"I've received a call from Kaiser Hospital in Santa Clara that Allen's father was taken there. I'm on my way to the Emergency Room . . ."

"Oh, my God!"

My knees were shaking though my tone stayed calm. "Would you please ask Allen to meet me there?"

"I shall," Flo answered. "I can reach him right away."

Oakland was miles of freeways away from Santa Clara. I knew Trish's office was nearby, so I dialed her number but was told she was out to lunch. Not wanting to leave an emergency message at the receptionist's desk alerting the whole staff, I left word for Trish to call Flo as soon as she returned.

Darting like a hunted squirrel, I searched for an executive to say I was leaving, but there were none and the president's secretary was still out to lunch. Abandoning everything on my desk, I swept my blazer from the back of the chair, grabbed my purse from the drawer and like a zombie alerted to an approaching enemy ran into the blistering August outdoors. I wanted to be air lifted to the hospital; the eight-mile distance loomed like a tortoise voyage to Mars. Calm down, I told myself, do one thing at a time. I fumbled the lock, jumped into the steaming car, placed my purse on the passenger seat, clicked the

Chapter 10

safety belt shut as my knees jerked as if plugged into an electric socket.

What to do next. Put the key in the ignition. I turn the key. The motor begins to whir, and the radio comes on. I switch the radio off. What now? Calm down, take a deep breath. One thing at a time, I again remind myself, or you'll never get there.

On to the frenetic lunch-hour California traffic where vehicles from all sides race by in a contest of see-how-close-you-can-cut in front of the other driver.

How did the hospital know where to find me? A couple of weeks earlier I'd made a wallet card for us with a list of emergency numbers but Jake wouldn't carry it. We're not listed in the phone book yet, I'd argued. He'd still refused to carry it. So Jake must've given the emergency people my office number, I reason, he must be lucid. The nurse said they were working on him. He's probably joking with the doctors and nurses. Keep your mind on Jake's jokes. I love Jake's jokes.

Turn on the radio. No, turn it off. Which joke do I love best? Can't remember any. Don't get too close to the car ahead. Am I keeping enough distance? Cars cutting in and out of my lane like miniatures on a child's electric race tracks make me feel as if I'm in a slow-motion movie scene, while everything around me is on fast-forward.

What time is it? I glare at the dashboard but nothing registers. Finally, there's the stoplight in front of the hospital. I turn in and move to where a sign says Emergency Entrance. There's an ambulance parked right in front. I pause. Where do I leave my car? Can't find a spot. Not one spot for me to park. I move on.

Round and round I circle, in a labyrinth jammed with stationary autos. No parking space. Anywhere.

In the distance, I recognize a security officer in a green go-cart looping around a corner. Moving to the center of the drive I come to a complete stop, hit a brief toot on the horn and rolling my window down stretch my head out. The officer speeds up and pulls up close. "Sir, I was called to the Emergency Room" I manage, "but can't find a place to park."

"Oh," he twists around pointing back, "you can park right in front of the Emergency entrance." I stare at him. The entrance could be any pinhole in that maze. "Why don't you follow me?" he suggests. Faltering, I trail his zigzag back to Emergency.

He passes by the ambulance still blocking the entrance and pulls over on the right side. Now, what do I do? Unfolding his big frame, the officer ambles over to my open window and leaning down to my eye-level, points to a space behind his vehicle. "Just leave your car there ma'am. It'll be fine." I ease my vehicle over and stumbling out slam my door shut and dash to the entrance where the automatic doors swing open welcoming me into its air-conditioned sanctum.

Inside, I scan the hushed lobby which appears to have a small reception area. My high-heeled pumps click-click-clicking on the glossed tile, I march to where a young woman is draped on a stool on the other side of a high desk. She looks up with a curious stare. Smile, I think to myself as my guts tighten, that'll make things right. "I received a call that my husband's here," I say. "I'm Lisa Saddler."

She doesn't smile back. Without saying anything to me, she swivels and shouts, "She's heeere," then spins back with a hint of I-know-something-you-don't and continues scanning the papers on her desk as if I were invisible. In the back hallway a side door opens and a mature, slim woman in a crisp white uniform and an erect posture, her dark short curls neatly arranged under a nurse's brief cap, strides over. At the entrance by the receptionist she says, "Mrs. Saddler?"

"Yes."

Chapter 10

"I'm Carol Thompson. I'm the one who called you." Her face is solemn. "Would you please follow me," she says, avoiding my eyes. Slipping through the doorway, I plod behind her through extended corridors into a small beige room. It's vacant. "Would you please wait here." Carol points to a tan vinyl sofa.

I remain standing. "Isn't he here? I'd like to see him." I search her guarded eyes.

"Yes, he's here." Her expression is blank. "Dr. Aaron will be with you." She turns toward the door.

"Do you need my insurance card?" I offer, digging in my purse.

"No that won't be necessary," she says lightly touching my hand. "Please sit down." I press the shaking card back in my billfold and stare at her. I don't want to sit down. I want to get to Jake's side. Why would she think I want to sit down? She slips out and gently closes the door behind her.

I start to pace.

I have to see him. Where is he? Why won't they take me to him? I put my purse on the couch and start to take my blazer off, but my body is chilled, so I shrug it back on. Like a caged tiger captured from the wild, I circle that windowless, colorless prison. From the couch to the other wall, to the corner desk and back again, my pleated skirt whirling around my wobbly knees. How long are they going to be? How long have I been here? I study my watch. Can't seem to focus on the time.

The door opens. An olive-skinned, chestnut wavy-haired young man in a starched doctor's smock with a stethoscope dangling around his neck saunters in and pushes the door shut behind him. "Mrs. Saddler?"

"Yes?"

"I'm Doctor Merced," he says extending a hand, then nervously pushing his glasses up. "I just have a few questions for you." He's so businesslike.

"Where is he?" I demand.

Dr. Merced stares at the floor. "He's here." Well then, why isn't he taking me to him—questions can wait till later. "Had he been sick?" Dr. Merced continues.

I take a step closer. "No. He was fine. He was in the shower when I left this morning."

"Had he had any problems before?"

Problems? I've got to think about that. "What kind of problem?"

"Any problems at all."

"No." Can't remember anything serious. "Not really." All I care about is now—who remembers yesterday? "How's he doing?" I'm through with trying to mask my impatience. This guy must be an intern. Young and inexperienced. I want to push him down to the floor and demand that he take me to Jake.

"Dr. Aaron will be with you shortly. Why don't you sit down," he says pointing to the couch." Sit down? I want to seize this Dr. Merced by the shoulders and shake him till his head bobs back and forth. I need to see my husband, and he's telling me to sit down? What kind of a doctor is he? And where is Dr. Aaron?

"No, thank you" I snap, stepping back. If I knew which room he's in, I'd go find him myself. Perhaps I'll just go and open every door in this building. Dr. Merced studies his shoes, then turns around and fumbles out. There's a phone on the built-in desk. I dial my office and ask the receptionist to tell my boss where I am and begin pacing again.

The door opens. Good, they'll finally take me to my Jake. I snatch my purse. A band of men and women, their eyes focused on the floor, file in silently like a black-and-white television commercial of creatures from another planet. In the wall-to-wall white-coated crowded space I recognize nurse Carol, who wedges herself by my side. A tall, middle-aged man with a clean-cut oval face and a mop of short gray hair bends his lean

Chapter 10

body over and grips my hand tightly. "Mrs. Saddler, I'm Dr. Aaron," he announces ever so soothingly.

Finally, someone's going to tell me. I search Dr. Aaron's clouded face. "How's he doing?"

"We've been working on him for an hour-and-half," he says very softly, his gentle, sensitive brown-velvet eyes padlocking mine. "He didn't have a pulse when they brought him in."

I wait to hear more. My brain isn't functioning.

"We've been trying to get a pulse. Unfortunately we haven't been successful," Dr. Aaron apologizes. Well, why don't you all go back and continue working on him instead of standing here doing nothing. Is anyone with him now? Please, please get back there, he'll respond. "It was a massive heart attack." Dr. Aaron is sympathetic.

I have to focus on this pulse business. A pulse. A pulse. Does that mean they picked up his wrist and couldn't find his pulse? Did they try the neck? Did they try anywhere else? What is a massive heart attack?

Dr. Aaron clutches my other hand and leaning closer whispers, "I'm sorry." His troubled eyes glistening with sadness bore through my iron shield exploding a cavernous hole in my soul.

Is this it? Is this all they're going to tell me? Does I'm Sorry mean they couldn't revive my Jake? Does I'm Sorry mean he's gone? He can't be. He was alive. In the shower. Talking to me, when I left this morning.

The people in white are simply standing around. This place is so suffocating, I'm going to pass out. The walls begin to rotate. I search for a place to sit. With one arm at my back, Dr. Aaron leads me to the couch and I plop down still holding on to his hand. Poor guy, he's so sad. They're all so somber. All they have to do is go back and keep working on my man. How come they're all hanging around here?

I catch Dr. Aaron's deep, dark, dejected eyes. "This is not easy for you," I tell him. My head sways. Where have I heard that? It was a woman. Those same words: "This is not easy for you." Flash! Of course, Donna Reed in *"The Best Place to Be,"* the movie Jake and I watched that Memorial Day evening in Minneapolis. The night Jake's soul urged that I remember his oracle.

Everyone has disappeared except Dr. Aaron and the nurse. "Carol will help you here," Dr. Aaron is saying. "Is there anyone you'd like to call?"

Call. Call. Oh yeah, call on the phone. "Yes, there is. I've already called my son and daughter-in-law. But I'd like to see my husband."

"Yes, you may. By law we have to call the coroner. He's on his way. Carol will stay with you." Slowly Dr. Aaron stands up. "I'm *so* sorry," he hesitates gazing down at me, then turns around and leaves.

I can't breathe. You have to stay in control, I tell myself. Don't buckle. Can I trust myself to see him alone and not break down? No, I must stay calm until the kids get here. "I'd like to wait and see him when my son or daughter-in-law arrive," I tell Carol.

"That will be okay," she agrees, sitting by my side.

I hunt for the telephone list I carry in my purse. "I've got to call my son in Chicago."

"I'll dial the number for you," Carol offers.

Unfolding the blue address sheet, I point to Marc's office number. Carol dials, then stretches the receiver toward me. I ease up and lean against the wall. Kate, Marc's secretary, is on the line. "I'm sorry, Marc's at a client meeting," she says.

Trying to keep my voice steady, I say, "I'm his mother in California. This is an Emergency. Could he please be called out?"

"Yes. Of course Mrs. Saddler. I'll get him right away." I grip the receiver tightly.

"Mom, Hi," I hear Marc say.

Chapter 10

My chest feels as if it has caved in. Slowly, precisely I say, "Marc, I'm calling you from the Emergency Room of Kaiser Hospital, in Santa Clara. Your father had a heart attack. Take the next plane out." Please God, don't let him ask me how he is.

"How's he doing?"

Stay in control. Stay in control. You can't break down now, and don't tell him he's already dead. "It's massive." What does that mean? It's the phrase the doctor used. "Marc, just see how soon you can get here."

"I'll be there as soon as I can Mom. How can I reach you?"

How can he reach me. "This hospital is very near our home. But, if you can't get us, call my office. They'll know how to find me."

"Okay Mom. I'll try to take the next plane out," Marc says.

It's going to be an arduous trek to the West Coast. It's a good thing I wasn't forced to tell him that his father was not alive. Next, Carol dials my office. My boss isn't back from lunch, so I ask to speak to the Human Resource Manager who cheerfully says, "Hi Lisa, this is Neil."

"Neil. My husband Jake is gone. I will not be back." Flash! "Sean is gone, Mother," that was what Donna Reed had said. In that movie. That Memorial Day.

"Lisa, what do you mean, He's gone?" Neil's asking.

I have to catch my breath. "I'm at the Kaiser Hospital. Jake died of a heart attack. My desk is unlocked. Please tell Bill."

Tenderly, Carol takes the receiver and places it back. Who else should I call. Not yet Greg, he's already struggling with hepatitis. I point at Richard's oriental rugs store number. With calculated calm, I begin "Rich, this is Lisa. I'm calling you from Kaiser Hospital . . . "

"Oh, my God, what happened?"

"Jake was brought in to Emergency."

"Emergency?" he shouts.

My heart is racing fast. "Rich, listen. Jake's very bad. I need you guys here."

He calms down a little. "Val's home with the flu. But I'll get her right away and we'll be there. How is he?"

My lips begin to tremble. "Rich, just get here. I need you."

"How is he?" he yells. "Tell me how he is. Is he okay? Lisa, tell me."

"Just get here Rich. I'm in the Emergency wing. Ask for me."

"This is the Meditation Room," Carol volunteers.

Another nurse appears. "Your son is on the phone. We don't want to lose him."

"I'll take you there," Carol says holding on to my arm.

It's Allen. "Mom, how are you doing?" His low, dejected voice is barely audible.

Closing my eyes I gather all of my inner resources. "I'm okay." Mustn't break down. *Can't* break down.

"Is Trish there yet?"

"No, not yet." Carol's arm tightens around my back.

"Trish is on her way. And I'll be there in half an hour." I've never heard him sound so haunting.

"Okay," I hear my voice echo in my head. Thank God he didn't ask how his father is, I think, as Carol walks me back. I didn't know that Dr. Aaron had given him the news before they came to get me.

In the Meditation Room, tearless, I sit straight up at the edge of the couch wringing my handkerchief. My teeth are chattering as if plugged into an electric socket. Carol comes in. "Mrs. Saddler, the coroner is here and they have to do their job."

I don't understand. "What's that?"

"They have to take him away," she explains.

I jump to my feet. "No, no, they can't do that. Please wait," I plead. "My son said his wife should be here any minute. Please, I can't see him by myself." I can't break down now, before anyone gets here.

Chapter 10

"Okay." Carol leaves.

I begin to pace again. My chest is tight. My head is buzzing. My chin quivers uncontrollably. And every fleeting second seems like twenty-four hours.

The doorknob turns and very slowly the door eases open. I look up to see Trish's smiling face with a question in her eyes, and for a few seconds our gaze locks.

"He didn't make it," I sob.

"Oh no," she cries. "No, it can't be." And we fall into each others' arms.

Carol's standing by. "Would you like to see him now?" she asks.

Trish stares at me puzzled. "They've been waiting to take him away. They say that the coroner must take him," I explain.

"Why?" She turns to Carol.

"It's the law. When a person expires who has not seen a physician within the past two months."

"Okay," Trish agrees. "We'll go see him now. But, you mustn't move him until his son gets here."

With Carol holding on to my one arm and Trish the other, we enter a stark, still, sanitized chamber. Jake's lying on a table with a tube in his nostril. His eyes are closed. His forehead is so white. He's so, so very, very still. The walls begin to oscillate.

Later, Trish and I wander out. Carol and some men in white are waiting. "Please hold him until his son arrives," Trish urges.

We're told Marc's on the phone. "I'll be arriving at eleven forty-five your time in San Francisco tonight, Mom," he says.

"Okay. Someone will meet you."

"Allen and I will," Trish offers.

"Mom, how's Dad doing?" I waiver. Should he be told before starting that long journey? I can't make decisions any more. I hand the receiver to Trish and steal away.

Allen arrives looking ashen. Clasping hands, dry-eyed, the three of us follow a nurse to the holding room. The physical body looks like my Jake, but his face is devoid of all color. What's happened to his rosy cheeks? He's so motionless. I stroke back his hair, caress his cheeks, bend down and kiss his forehead.

Later, with Allen's arm around my waist and Trish hanging on to his hand, we stumble away.

"I want to spend the night with him," I say.

"You can't, Mom."

Who says I can't? "Yes, I can. I want to." I've got to.

"You can't Mom. It's the law. The coroner has to take him away."

"Where?" This is our man, not theirs.

"Mom, they'll let us know when they can release him."

A nurse shows Richard and Valerie in. "Where is he? Where is he?" Rich is screaming, bouncing around staring from me to Allen to Trish.

"Rich, sit down . . ." I take his arm.

He shrugs me away. "No. I'm not sitting down. Where is he? Take me to him." Lunging at Allen he bellows, "I want to see him. He's not gone is he? He can't be gone. We were together this Sunday."

I rush out to seek help and find Carol. "You've got to do something," I beg. "My brother's hysterical. He's a diabetic." A doctor appears, sits down by Richard and takes his pulse.

From Carol, Allen takes a couple of white pills and a Styrofoam cup with water. "Here Mom, take this, will you," he murmurs.

Carol then strides back with a large white plastic bag emblazoned "Patient Belongings." She hands Allen the bag which I suspect contains Jake's clothes, and from a brown envelope pulls out Jake's wallet and keys.

"Do they know where Dad's car is?" Allen asks.

Chapter 10

Extending a piece of paper, Carol explains, "This is the number you are to call. It's the Athletic Club. He was brought here from there."

"Trish," Allen says, turning to her, "I'll meet you guys at Mom's. We'll come back and pick up my car later." He puts his arm around me. "Come on Mom, let's go home."

In that drag to an empty apartment, I keep biting my lips to stop the quivering. Allen pulls into our parking stall, comes around unbuckles my seat belt, helps me out. Trudging up the steps to my home of less than nine months, we hang on to each other.

Inside, whiffs of roses dance their welcome as Allen gathers me in his arms. Finally, I can let go. He was my husband, he was my lover, he was the father I never had. He was my best friend. "I'm not going to make it," I weep.

"Yes, you are Mother, you're going to make it," Allen whispers, as our quivering bodies cleave to each other.

I remember hearing somewhere, A death ends a life but not a relationship.

Chapter 11

Shadows of the Moonlight

Those who knew Jake agreed that he died exactly the way he would have chosen: on his feet. That noon at the health club, he was batting the ball alone on the racquetball court when an instructor suggested they play a game together. As they were to start keeping score, Jake told his partner, "I feel dizzy, give me a minute." He eased down on the floor and keeled over.

The instructor's immediate resuscitation efforts expounded by ambulance paramedics on their streak to Emergency, plugged him into state-of-the-art life-saving methodology for over an hour before the jarring pronouncement. Hospital administrative personnel had traced me through the insurance card in Jake's billfold, issued by the medical clinic we had joined two months earlier.

We had a private family funeral followed by an open memorial service, and a reception at home where our anniversary roses still dazzled in a flourish of flowers kindled with condolence cards. Jeanne and Dennis, who less than ten months earlier had flown in to toast Allen and Trish's wedding, returned for a rueful good-bye. "Don't make any decisions for a year," Dennis advised as they were leaving. "Give yourself time."

In our raw immediacy of shock and sorrow, Marc and Allen, a beacon of caring and understanding, took charge of details and legalities. Marc stayed with me fielding phone calls.

It was weeks after the funeral, when I allowed myself to recall the dream I had rejected that Thursday which shattered my earth.

Chapter 11

On the eighth morning following Jake's death, I awakened to sounds of Marc preparing breakfast in the kitchen, fused with the low murmur of traffic bouncing in from my open window. At just before six, the Northern California sun was still low in the east. As I hesitated between going back to sleep or getting up to join Mark, a changed aura obliterated the familiar sounds demanding my attention. And my bedroom began to reverberate with a pulsing beat like the tom, tom, tom, of a muffled drum.

Still not fully alert, trying to determine how an undulating pulse could pound my space, lazily I opened my eyes. Jake was standing at the far end of the foot of our bed. Since the start of day was the most painful part of adjustment, thinking I was fantasizing, I closed my lids, focused on my surroundings, and reopened my eyes. Jake was still standing there, appearing to be preoccupied with getting dressed as if it were just another ordinary work day. His upper body leaning slightly forward to get a good look in the dresser mirror, he was absorbed with buttoning his crisp, white, long-sleeved dress shirt.

For a few seconds, I watched mystified. All sounds of the planet earth had disappeared but everything in our bedroom was the same. It's Jake . . . but why is he doing that?

As if I'd spoken out loud, still preoccupied with getting dressed, Jake signaled that he had an appointment, or some kind of an interview, and it was important that he keep his commitment. The communication was normal, much like talk between husband and wife without eye contact, in the morning hustle of getting ready for work.

Puzzled, I continued to stare. What is happening here? Picking up my confusion, Jake abruptly stopped, and in the flicker of an eyelash wasn't standing up any more. He was sitting on the blue velveteen rocker facing our bed; his spine resting against the cushioned back with his legs stretched out his shoulders hunched forward, very still, focusing on a distant horizon.

This is definitely a physical person. I know Jake is physically dead, so this can't be Jake. Richard is alive. Can it be Richard sitting there?

Slowly, like a maestro acknowledging his audience, the head moved up, turned and faced me. And, for the first time, looked directly at me challenging recognition. I scrutinized the entity very, very cautiously.

No question. It was Jake.

But, he's dead. How can he be here when he's dead?

Our gaze interlocked in a bombshell of reality. Deliberately, lingeringly, through thought transfer I said, "You don't have to go through that any more Jake. You're dead." In less than the flash of a wink, the physical form disappeared—gone. Vaporized. And I was left staring at an empty armchair.

Sounds from the kitchen and outside traffic, filled the void.

I was dazed. I heard a deep sigh escape from the depth of my being. Jake wasn't aware of his physical death until I told him. Pins and needles began to go up and down my spine. Unsteadily, I got up, put my robe on, and shuffled out to the kitchen.

"Mom, I made breakfast for us," Marc said then stopped, searching my eyes with a troubled gaze. "Are you okay?"

I sat down. "Your dad was just in my bedroom."

Marc sat by my side. "He was? I wish I could've seen him," he whispered, for he and Allen had grown up accepting as normal what others called paranormal. Marc and his dad were close, with a special bond that had gotten tighter with the years. In his last undergraduate year, he and Jake had even taken a spring vacation trip to the Caribbean together.

Calmly, I described what had transpired.

"Do you think Dad had an appointment that we need to cancel?" he asked.

"I don't know."

"Could he have reserved a plane or something?"

I couldn't find Jake's appointment book, so we checked with his flying club. He hadn't reserved a plane. Later we got a call

Chapter 11

from his ophthalmologist to be reminded of an eye exam the following afternoon.

Daybreak was the worst: having to come to terms, all over again, with the irreversibility of death. Many times, I'd catch myself wishing the day Jake died could simply be annulled. Thursday the 13th—erased from the calendar. Then life would ingeniously return to normalcy.

At my request, Marc contacted Bill, my boss, suggesting that, since I couldn't make a commitment about a return date, he hire another assistant. Getting back to work would be good therapy, Bill proposed; he'd hold the position open for me for as long as it took.

Marc left for his home in Chicago. I returned to the office after over a two-week absence, determined I'd not use any euphemisms. No "passed on." Died . . . Died. That's what happened. My husband died. No longer with me. He was dead.

On Friday evening, when I entered our apartment the fragrance of fresh roses was staggering. Reasoning that the boys must have had some flowers delivered, I put my purse in the kitchen and peeked at the dining room table. No flowers. I went into the living room. No flowers. Were they in the bedrooms? No, there were no flowers there either. The windows were closed against the August heat outside, the draperies drawn, the apartment silent.

Okay, I resolved, I'm going to ignore this and have something to eat; it must be in my mind. But it wasn't in my mind. Like the steady waves of an ocean, whiffs of the fragrance wafted around me.

In my research of the paranormal, I'd come across cases of confrontation with overpowering intimately-meaningful aromas after a death, but had totally forgotten about it until that evening. In addition to Jake's first tribute to me of roses (way back there in Africa), he'd always been very generous with bouquets of fresh flowers. Often, he'd approach me with one arm behind his back, eyes fired with a secret like a little boy's. "I smell flowers," I'd sing out, and he'd extend his offering.

That night in bed, I tossed and turned. Jake had been my greatest supporter of receiving spiritual messages through automatic writing. Now, if I didn't give it a try, it was as if I were ignoring his need to communicate. After a great deal of meditation, I reached for my writing pad.

"Jake," I wrote, "where are you?"

The tip of the pen quivered and stopped. I took a deep breath, held firmly to the pen, affirming, "I let go, and let peace." The pen began to quiver again. Then, slowly, shakily, it started to move.

"My soul is with you."

I had to find out about his appearance.

"That morning, were you aware that you were in my room and I talked with you?"
"We were together for a long time before you knew it was me."
"Are you happy?"
"Yes I am very happy. I am with all of you and helping you all the time."
"Do you remember having any pain?"
"My heart stopped and love took over."
"Have you seen Mother and Mary?"
"Yes. The angels took me to them. For a while I didn't know what happened. My body was still like my old body when I was with you."
"When did you understand what had happened?"
"When you said that I was dead."

Chapter 11

"When you were here, did you suspect you were having a heart problem?"

"*I knew that my heart was not right, but I didn't think it was much to be concerned about. I didn't want to worry you, so I pretended that I didn't want to be very active.*"

On the morning of his death, Jake had called Allen after I'd left. But they'd only discussed some repairs Allen was having done on his house. I thought about that telephone call now, and before I wrote down anything, the pen continued:

"*You were concerned that the boys wouldn't be around when we needed them. I wanted to tell Allen that he and you would need each other, to stay close to home if he could. But didn't.*

"*We are growing here . . . I feel as if I haven't changed, just become more tuned to nature. I have a new body and it's so good to be in this one. It is like flying without an airplane.*"

At pre-dawn five weeks after Jake's death, the skies were still dark when I became engulfed in a peaceful reverie as if a full moon had suddenly surfaced on a crisp, clear night. Sensing a familiar presence, I opened my eyes and focused on Jake standing by the side of the bed about four feet away. I wasn't startled; only curious. His eyes dancing with pride, his body radiating a gentle rhythm of earth-sense as if he had crawled back into his material form, his telepathic contact vibrated with love. I recognized it was my Jake—not that I could see details of his physical features, but because of the glow of his unique individual soul.

As soon as I acknowledged him, like a 5-year-old proud of a hard-to-win victory, flinging that sheepish grin he signaled, "Here I am!"

Here you *are*? What are you doing here?

"I've been waiting for you to wake up and recognize me. See?" he dazzled, as if activating an electronic flare.

Why are you so proud of yourself?

"Well first, I'm here," he indicated. And I understood that he had to accomplish an intense amount of learning to be able to project himself on my plane.

Sadly I thought, Well, you're dead though, aren't you?

Patiently, he explained, "Yes, I'm physically dead." Then with an amplifying brilliance proudly added, "But, I did postpone my death, didn't I?" I tried to comprehend exactly what he meant. "You can't deny that," he asserted.

Now I understood. His death came nine months *after* the one-and-half years his soul message had signaled that Memorial Day. Of course I couldn't deny that! The warning had instigated our move to California, and Jake had willed himself to live until I was safely settled near Allen and Trish, and also until we celebrated our 30th wedding anniversary together.

Yes, I signaled. I understand. Thank you. Thank you.

Gratified that I absorbed his feat, Jake vanished. After instructing my subconscious to retain all details of the contact, I fell into a peaceful sleep.

The phenomena of postponing imminent physical death is borne out by families who see a terminal loved one miraculously extend life, in many cases until the completion of a specific goal. In his awe inspiring book *The Wisdom of the Body,* Dr. Sherwin B. Nuland, Yale's distinguished surgeon and bioethicist, author of award-winning *How We Die,* acknowledges that many times the patient's will to live has nullified medical prognosis of physiological termination.

Chapter 11

I tried. I tried to concentrate on our good life together for over thirty years, but the pain of his absence overwhelmed all my senses. In my journal I wrote:

> To outsiders, one appears to function normally, but the sinking feeling that is almost always now present, eliminates all motivation that once animated the desire to live and achieve a goal. I know that I've been given so much, but it is still very hard for me to make sense, to accept life as worth pursuing.
>
> A lot of times I feel so much is beyond my understanding, my ability to put the jigsaw puzzle together to come out with a pattern that spells Truth. I do know that the physical energy form we called Jake is continuing, but my frustration at this level is my inability to make contact at will. The three levels of contact are very clear to me, but the variables which impact communication appear insurmountable for he's only appeared to me twice.
>
> I know that if it were possible for Jake to do so, he would communicate with me more than he has done so far. Today, six weeks after his physical death, my non-written communication is not occurring at a level that I can duplicate at will. Or that I can continue, when it does suddenly happen.
>
> Physical image communication appears to be instantaneous, and disappears immediately when I become aware that I've made contact.
>
> Not now, but I know that some day, the human species will evolve to a spiritual/chemical level where the kinds of surprise contacts I have experienced will be created at will.

Not quite two months after Jake's death, I was changing my bed one evening when, through an opening between the mattress and headboard, I saw a yellow slip of paper on the carpet. I crawled under the bed, and dragged it out. It was a yellow 5½"×4" pre-printed telephone message form used in businesses. The writing was Jake's, in red ink. It said:

To: *Lisa*

Date: *Now*
Time: (blank)
Message: *I LOVE YOU*

I turned it over; the back was blank. I flopped on the bed, read it again and again and again. Holding it in my palms, through deep breathing I stilled my quivering body and calmed my racing mind wondering whether there might be an instant spiritual communication. But there was none.

Later that night, on my notepad I asked,

"Jake, when did you leave this note for me?"

After some scrambled lines, the pen moved . . .

"I wrote the note on August 13 and put it under your pillow."

"Did you know that you were going to leave your physical body that day? And why did you say 'Now' for the date?"

"I was not feeling very well, but I didn't know that my physical body would stop like that. I wrote 'I love you,' that you would know I always love you, whether you see me or not. **Now** *means always, whenever you think of me."*

"Do you remember anything else about the 13th of August?"

"I was not very sure that I'd be able to play racquetball, but thought I'd try. I cleaned the apartment and I wrote the note for you. We had just begun to start the game when I did not feel right, so I thought I'd rest a little. Then I felt that I was going on a long journey and that's when I thought that I may not be able to continue my game. But my body didn't feel different. I was merely very light and could do anything I wanted.

Chapter 11

"I want you to write that we never go on to a distant land. We are always near. You don't see us because we are not in our physical bodies."

"Why do you disappear as soon as I realize that it's you."

"I am not sure yet . . . I'm learning, and there is very much to learn."

One morning I woke up feeling very peaceful. Everywhere, I felt Jake's mischievous, relaxed presence following me around as he often did when on this plane. It was only after I arrived at the office, that I remembered it was the day I was to transfer the title of my Mustang. My stomach somersaulted, my knees tottered. Jake had surprised me with the auto for our 24th wedding anniversary. Now, I was going to have to say good-bye to a vault that held a myriad of memories.

I got a flashback of the evening a group of us rushed to our garage to view the new hardtop Jake had just driven home. Close friends David and Maureen were with us for an outdoor barbecue, with their house guest (a natural-born storyteller commercial pilot) who entertained us with tales of his escapades in the air.

That summer, Allen, home from college, was working with his father in Cleveland, both commuting weekends to Orchard Park, New York, where Marc and I remained until the sale of our home. Scouting for a car to replace my old one, Jake and Allen had come across a sleek, just-off-the-line, ruby red, Mustang II.

"You've got to buy this, Dad. It's perfect for Mom. She'll love it," 20-year-old Allen urges.

After a test drive, his father says, "I've got to think about it."

"What do you mean, you've got to think about it," Allen protests. "This is fabulous! We haven't seen anything like it. If you don't buy it now, someone's going to snatch it away, Dad."

The next afternoon, when Allen is working in the field with the construction crew, Jake goes back, buys the car, and instructs that it be placed in the back lot with a large "SOLD" sign.

After dinner, Jake says to Allen: "What do you think? Shall we go by and take a second look at that Mustang?"

"Yes, yes," Allen jumps up. "Let's go. You've got to buy it before it's sold, Dad. I know it's going to go fast. I *know* it is."

They get in Jake's car and drive to the dealership. "There it is," Allen shouts. "There it is. That's the one." Jake stops the car. "But it's sold," Allen realizes, leaping out. "Oh Dad, it's already sold." Jake strolls over. "Somebody's bought it," Allen shakes his head. "I told you we'd lose it if we didn't snap it up yesterday. You never listen to me, Dad. Never!"

Extending his closed fist, then calmly spreading his fingers to reveal the keys, Jake says to his son, "Here. Would you like to drive your mother's new car?"

"Oh, Dad. You did it again."

Six years later, after handing over those keys to a colleague who had bought the car for her 20-year-old son, I rushed into the bathroom to weep. I can't cope, I thought. Then I remembered: on especially trying days, Jake's presence became an invisible companion.

One Friday, returning from a late lunch break at around one-thirty, the song *Blue Moon* wafted from my car radio. This is 1981—nobody plays that song any more. Jake's favorite, he used to sing *Blue Moon* to me when we started falling in love thirty-two years ago.

> Blue Moon, you saw me standing alone
> Without a dream in my heart,
> Without a love of my own.

Chapter 11

> Blue Moon, you knew just what I was there for
> You heard me saying a pray'r for
> Someone I really could care for.

The following Friday, I was returning from the bank when "Blue Moon" came on the radio again. I noted the time: 1:38 p.m. As soon as I reached the office, I called the program manager of the station. "Oh, it's probably on the new tape," he explained, "which would mean that it would be played once every ten days. But not in the same time-slot. We never play the same song at the same time."

In my journal I wrote:

It is almost seven weeks since Jake's death. I miss him so terribly much that I get nauseated when I think of him. I wonder how long this sinking feeling in my stomach will go on. I feel so removed from reality. I'm lackadaisical, and consider everything in life mundane and unimportant.

When I am motivated to be active I begin to realize how much I miss him. When I am not motivated, I have no feeling whatsoever; no interest in what's going on, and I don't want to go on living.

Without the nurturing warmth of my Jake's presence, my world of sunshine has now been hurled into an unexpected limbo, and my familiar former comfortable existence has turned into an unfamiliar harsh reality.

Learning to live without my love of thirty-two years feels like learning to walk. Almost makes me feel that I'm a little incapable child who is learning to take first steps again, venturing out into an unknown world. That is really frightening.

I braced myself to go through Jake's personal belongings to give them away. In his top dresser drawer, I discovered a recent pink Lab Services Request form made out in Jake's name from our medical clinic.

I didn't remember Jake saying that he had undergone any lab tests. I didn't remember being billed for any lab services. I did recall Jake going in to have some tingling at the end of his fingers checked. He had come back with some vials of sample drugs. That evening he said, "I don't care for that Dr. Lawrence."

"We can switch doctors in the clinic any time we want, you know. If you don't like Dr. Lawrence, why don't you switch to someone else?" I'd suggested.

"I'll think about it," Jake had calmly replied, as he lay on the couch reading the paper.

I went over and sat by his side. "Exactly what did he say?" I asked as he laid the newspaper down and scooted over to give me more room.

"Oh, he said that chances are it's not anything serious. He gave me those samples to try out for a while."

"What are they for?"

"They're an anti-inflammatory compound. He said that, basically, it's aspirin, but perhaps twenty times stronger."

"Is that all?"

He held my hand in his. "Yeah, that's all." Jake hated the thought that he might not be well, so I didn't want to sound alarmed or make him think I was pressuring him.

Now, I stared at the pink Lab Request form with three items circles. I eased on the bed and dialed the clinic. I identified myself and asked to talk to Dr. Lawrence.

"What's this in connection with?" his nurse said.

"It's in connection with my husband, Jake Saddler."

"I'm sure Dr. Lawrence would be happy to talk with Mr. Saddler," she said.

Hugging his pillow to still my spastic knees, I said, "I'm sorry, he's not available right now, and I need to speak with the doctor about a personal matter."

"Just a minute," she answered. "I'll have to get his chart."

Chapter 11

When Dr. Lawrence came on the line, I explained to him that I couldn't find Jake's lab reports, only his medication for arthritis.

"Yes," he said. "I remember Jake. I did prescribe medication for arthritis. But I wanted him to undergo some lab tests. He needed to come back for those because they required that he fast. He didn't come back."

He didn't come back! Now curled into a fetal position, my shoulders weakened, my vision blurred. That was my Jake. If he didn't want to do something, in his quiet, passive manner he didn't do it.

Dr. Lawrence explained that he was concerned about Jake's smoking and also wanted to check his cholesterol level. "Naturally, I can't force any of my patients to take these tests," he emphasized. "I thought, perhaps, Jake had gone to another doctor."

"He didn't," I said softly.

"Jake and I had a long session together. He gave me details of his habits and his hobby of flying. He told me about his playing racquetball, which was good. But I did want to check out the side effects of smoking." Dr. Lawrence paused, then added, "If there's anything else that you might think of at any time, please feel free to call."

I couldn't speak. My chest felt caved in, my head pounded like hail hammering glass.

"How's he doing now?" I heard Dr. Lawrence ask.

He doesn't know that Jake died! That dolorous day, his clinic had supplied the hospital my office phone number, but must not have recorded anything on his chart. My throat felt like the Sahara Desert. I swallowed hard. "Jake had a fatal heart attack while playing racquetball two months ago," I managed. My voice echoed as if it belonged to someone else far, far away.

"I'm so sorry, Mrs. Saddler," I heard Dr. Lawrence's hushed reply. I dug my head under Jake's pillow and wailed.

In 1981, the medical profession was only at the beginning of assessing the incendiary nature of tobacco.

Soon after we were married, Jake asked if I'd like him to quit smoking. At the time I'd said, No, it didn't matter. Later, after the destructive properties of smoking became public knowledge, I refused to buy cigarettes for him as I once had done. I'd even pointed out, "Jake, if you want to shorten your life it's your decision. But I'm not going to help you."

Occasionally, as I'd be getting ready to go to the store, he'd probe, "Oh, would you get me a carton of 'so-and-so'."

"You know I won't Jake."

"Well, they're filtered. And they're low tar. They really aren't heavy on nicotine."

"I won't," I'd glare.

When Jeanne and Dennis's son, Kevin Barton, was preparing to graduate from high school, Dennis, a very heavy smoker, was in the hospital with terminal lung cancer. His prognosis was grim: three to six months. I flew out to see Dennis and to be with Jeanne and Kevin for the graduation.

Dennis, who at one time was a 220 lb. hunk, had now, at 57, deteriorated into a gaunt shadow. Perched side by side clasping hands, surrounded by an oasis of humming electronic monitors we reminisced about the adventures he and Jeanne and Jake and I had sailed through as an extended family.

Then Dennis became serious and started to talk about smoking. In a voice now hardly above a murmur, he explained. "Lisa, when Jake and I were growing up, at every break in high school we ran to the back of the grocery store to sneak a smoke. Everybody did it, and of course you didn't want to be left out. Who knew we would be hooked then?"

Who knew?

Chapter 11

The weeks inched by. Officially, the calendar said Fall, which in Northern California is the beginning of the rainy season. I agreed to care for Allen and Trish's two kittens, Ozzie and Harriet, when they were going to be out of town for a brief vacation. Two rambunctious, lively kittens, who especially delighted at jumping up and knocking over a potted ficus plant. So at bedtime, they were confined to snoozing together in a closed bathroom.

One night, awakened by the rumblings of a winter rainstorm, I checked on Ozzie and Harriet who appeared fine, and returned to bed. Sinking down under my comforter, I listened to the winds howl and the thunder roll, until eventually the raging chaos shifted to a monotonous downpour. As I became drowsy, and my eyelids weighted down, I sensed a charged aura which had nothing to do with the storm. Abruptly awake, I scooted up on my pillows wondering whether the kittens may have gotten out, or were squabbling in the bathroom. They weren't.

The rhythm of the rain on the roof was constant, and my home safe. In the limited night shadows everything looked normal and in place, but enveloped in a changed environment, my apartment felt as if it were magnetized in a suspended timeless "pause" zone as if I were hit by an invisible lightening. Not a destructive electrical current. Harmless. But potent, much like utter silence after an explosion.

Suddenly, I was no longer alone. Jake, looking exactly as he did when alive, was sitting next to me on the bed.

I'd thought I'd never see him physically again. Jake, Jake's here, my whole entity screamed. And so close. We were always tactile, clasping our fingers, reaching for each other in the car, watching TV lounging in each others' arms. Now, to be sure, I needed to feel his body. Stretching over, I touched his chest lightly with my right hand. My God, he feels so solid, I thought, exactly like a living, breathing physical body.

Fully aware that Jake was physically dead I glided my hand up to his shoulder, pivoting around and resting my other hand on his thigh. As my heart raced I announced, "Jake, Jake it's you, you're here." I wanted to get close. I wanted to touch and feel all of him. But before lunging forward, I thought I needed permission. "Can I please hug you?" I requested.

He signaled, "No."

I kept my hands where they were, savoring the firmness of his body. Okay, I won't hug you. I'll only hold on. I'm happy simply holding on.

The body started to become faint. "Oh Jake, you're fading away. Please don't go, please don't go," I pleaded. The form reassembled in less than the wink of an eyelash. Partially removed, as calm and serene as an evening sunset, Jake sat there gazing at me. Certainly not as ecstatic as I was. Telepathically, I got the message that he was waiting for me to truly comprehend that he was with me, and this was the most ultimate way he could prove that there was an ongoing part of him.

As if pre-programmed he started to fade, and I begged, "Oh, please don't go. Please!" The physical form became clearer. Then reaching over, very, very gently, as light as the touch of a butterfly, without saying anything, he gave me a kiss on my right cheek.

He was gone. The magnetic atmosphere lingered.

Now what happens? I needed to go to the bathroom, but was paralyzed with fear, for I'd never presumed it possible to be plunged into the type of physical communication in an electromagnetic aura that had materialized. What if I were confronted by other spirits alien to me? I lay immobile in the throbbing panorama.

Soon, a calmness like an evening breeze saturated me, and I lay back against the pillows until gradually the electromagnetic currents waned into normal earth vibrations. I slid down under the comforter and fell asleep.

In reviewing all parapsychological research I could locate, I discovered that electric storm activity has often clearly heightened psychic sensitivity.

Most scientists agree that there are four dimensions: three Spatial, (relating to, occupying, or occurring in space) plus Time. Other scientists believe that there are only Latitude, Longitude and Altitude, with the fourth dimension as Time. Variables within our physical world such as velocity, acceleration, force, pressure, momentum, and pulsation create an extra dimension which (although not directly visible) affect the atmosphere in which we find ourselves.

I was in awe of having found myself in a magnetic field which promoted that level of communication, and I had no doubt that the physical person I loved now continued in an evolutionary form of energy. But that knowledge does not magically eradicate the pain of loss.

There was a letter from a friend which said, "Lisa, you are such an inspiration to all who know you." I'm not, I thought. Deep down inside I hurt. I hurt very badly. People only see my superficial veneer and take for granted that I can handle sorrow; I can't.

Focusing on keeping up the facade, "I'm doing well," I lied to my friends. "Yes, I'm fine," I insisted to my sons. And hoped they all believed me.

"It's not going to be easy, Lisa," Valerie said, "but you're strong."

Once, the president of our company stopped at my desk. "You're a very strong lady. You're going to make it," he said.

I was beginning to resent that word "strong." How did they assume I was strong? Inside, I was weak and miserable.

Fifty years ago when my mother had been widowed, she was not only expected to grieve but was encouraged to visibly mourn the loss of the father of her children. For forty days she had practically taken to her bed while female relatives prepared meals, welcomed guests who came to pay their condolences, and stayed to help with the children. She had worn black for a year. I wore white to my husband's funeral and asked that, in recognition of a return to the purity of spirit, my family also disregard black.

All that occurred when I was still in shock. The terrible ache of a loss, inherent in life on this planet earth, started to set in later. And the practical healing began when I joined a grief therapy group.

Chapter 12

Gentle Healings

For two months I combed libraries and bookstores searching for material to help ease my grief. There was very little I was unfamiliar with. One afternoon Eleanor, our Account Manager at the bank, called to tell me that a widowed friend of hers had been getting a great deal of comfort from group grief therapy meetings. "I was wondering if you might want to look into it," she suggested. At first I thought group grief support was not the answer, for I had access to a personal therapist. Later, assessing my options, I questioned whether anyone who's not had a major personal loss can truly fathom the fracture of death, and Eleanor's idea appeared more and more promising.

Once the super-daughter, super-wife, super-mother, super-friend, I was now desperately trying to become the super-widow; with only sporadic, external success. I realized that, though in the past I had had the tools to help myself and reach out to others, now I craved a nurturing, unthreatening support system dislodged from concerns about whether my grief was taxing my close-knit family.

Through our local hospital human resource director, I obtained a list of group support systems and contacted the office of a nearby recently established foundation created by a bright, successful woman who had had to cope with the death of several family members within a few short years. I was screened by phone, and designated to a group beginning Friday.

"What?" my boss exclaimed when I told him I couldn't work late on Fridays. "You don't need grief therapy."

Another vice president volunteered, "Go out with the gang for a beer after work. Get yourself a boyfriend and get away weekends. The Mark Hopkins has an excellent brunch on Sunday mornings. You should see the view."

"I've seen it," I said swiveling my chair away.

He sauntered around. "Well, see it again."

"Bruce, I've had all that."

"That doesn't mean you can't have it again," he pronounced. It hadn't even been two months. Did anyone really comprehend the urgency of sorrow?

The following Friday, I drove directly from the office to my first meeting. Was it going to be true what most people thought? That banding together to talk about death would be morbid. Was bereavement a subject one didn't openly dissect? And did that mean those who do are weak?

At the meeting center, with taped soft music in the background, petite, raven-haired Monica extended a firm handshake inviting us to get comfortable on the giant cheerful floor cushions. Her emerald eyes and vulnerable smile sweeping us into a cohesive gathering, 32-year-old Monica began the dialogue by outlining her own background. A trained grief counselor, she explained that although she was not grieving the death of a loved one, she was mourning the death of her marriage.

"Divorce is like a death," she pointed out, "a very painful loss. Divorce may even have an additional trauma. Rejection." Monica then proposed that going around the circle, we introduce ourselves and tell the group a little bit about our loss. There were eight of us—four widows, a widower, a single young woman and a married couple who were grandparents.

Long-limbed Stephanie, a Nordic blonde in her early 20s, her voice reflecting the tremor of an operatic aria said, "Evan, my fiancée, was killed by a drunk driver one month before we were going to be married. I was raised in a family where only the positive was stressed. I now realize that for the past two years

I've been fooling myself about everything being okay with me. It's not. I have to face the fact that I miss Evan terribly, and I want to mourn my dream that crumbled."

Slouching against her husband as he held her hand, the grandmother pressed her lips together then muffling a sob said, "Our granddaughter, Lauren, was only 3 when she was taken from us. It's so hard to see other children play. Or laugh. Or jump puddles. Or do all those things kids do." And he confessed, "We keep asking ourselves Why? Why would a child have to die of cancer?"

Another young widow, crossing and re-crossing her tanned legs sighed, "Next month it'll be the first-year's anniversary of Fred's death, and still I don't know what phase of grief I'm in. One day I'm angry for his dying. Another, I can't believe that he's gone. I recently started seeing other men. But, I feel guilty." She turned to Monica. "Should I even be thinking of other men? Should I have a time frame? When am I going to stop hurting?"

Monica stood up. "For the time being, remove the word 'should' from your vocabulary," she instructed, strolling to the board in the corner of the room. "Make it your highest priority to be patient with yourself." Grabbing a piece of chalk, she wrote: (1) I will not set limits on myself.

Twisting around, gazing at each of us she said, "Give yourself all the time you need to grieve." She then added: (2) I will not hurry my grief.

"Do only what you're equipped to do," Monica went on. "If you don't feel like having the family over, tell them. If you feel like going out, do so. You don't have to apologize for your grief—no matter how long it takes."

Creating a sub-list on the board of integral parts in our lives now snatched away from us, we identified: the treasure of the sound of their voice, the contagious mirth of their laughter, the intoxicating warmth of their love, the buoyancy of their understanding, the comfort of security, the companionship of sharing.

"Let's admit it," Monica declared with a sweep of her hand, "there is a lot we have lost. Haven't we?" It was such a relief being open about my pain.

Once, Dorothy, a widow in her 50s with a commanding presence who had nursed her husband with cancer stated, "I'm still so very angry. David wouldn't talk about his illness, or the fact that he was dying. Only once we cried together, and he later said, 'Now, we're not going to do this again.' I wanted to do that over and over again, share our suffering with each other, scream at the world." Ignoring the box within her reach, she jerked her purse open and pulled out several tissues. "You know what?" she asserted dabbing her cheeks, "Now, when I see older couples together I resent them. I keep thinking, we should have been doing that together. It's been over five years, and I'm still angry at him for leaving me. It's excruciating for me to live in the same house. His chair, the empty bed. Everything."

"Anger is a normal part of the grieving process," Monica pointed out. I remembered a recent evening when I arrived home through a stop-and-go tough commute, and began searching for Jake in the apartment thinking, *Okay Jake, I really do miss you—you've never stayed away this long before, come home, it's time that you came home now.* Then stumbled into the bedroom flinging myself on our bed shed buckets and buckets of tears. Another time, approaching our apartment I caught sight of a red pick-up truck with a driver wearing a crimson windbreaker. My heart thudded like a mallet at my ribs and my mind cheered: *There's my Jake in his flight jacket; he isn't dead, he's just been gone a while and he's now coming home.* I wanted to share my day with him. I wanted to get his feedback. I wanted his thoughts. I wanted his body against mine. In my journal I wrote:

Chapter 12

> I don't know when my brain is going to understand that death is irreversible. This is not an interim period away from Jake. This is the pattern of a life without him for the rest of my life, and I really do not want to go on living.

Friday evenings offered a glimmer of a flashlight in the dark, when I didn't have to veil my anguish. Meeting for at least two-hour sessions, the group provided non-judgmental, non-religious, empathetic support. Our numbers fluctuated, but the membership didn't change. I was the most recently bereaved.

At one meeting, pairing off we exchanged statements such as: I feel guilty about . . . My family doesn't understand because . . . One of the ways I help myself is . . . I will give myself the luxury of . . .

What sometimes nudged at me was whether I'd done enough for this man who'd always been loving and patiently considerate but not too verbal about his feelings. I adored him. But did I really demonstrate my love enough? Most of the time, I was the one who said "I love you" first, then he'd answer "I love you too." Stubbornly, sometimes I'd wait for him to say it first. Had I been too unyielding? Once, returning home from a gala New Year's Eve bash, we lay together enwrapped, talking until the snow outside shimmered with sunrise. I had broached the subject of verbalizing our feelings more often and he'd said, "Lisa, you know I'm not too good with talking about how I feel." I didn't have to quiz him, for this man had survived a miserably abused home life by tucking away his emotions in the depths of his exploited solitary childhood.

When we highlighted our guilt, Monica pointed out, "Confront your feelings and know that at the time you did the best you could. The fact that you realize you could have done better allows you to acknowledge you've learned from your mistakes. It's okay, learning is part of growing."

Early on in our sessions, Monica asked us to make a list of the most important elements in our life that we had now lost.

"What I miss most" I said, "is the anchor that was such a beautiful harbor for me, specially when I came home after the helter-skelter of the business world. Jake was such a calm, ethical, good person. A positive influence in all areas of my life." And Ron, the widower, nodded.

Monica prodded, "I didn't hear anything about their physical presence. What about the flesh and blood, their body just being there?"

Mirroring the ache in our bones, the grandfather mused, "That's so obvious to each of us, I guess we just took it for granted that it's a given." Shaking his head as if to anesthetize the pain, he reached for his forehead with quivering fingers scraping through his curly silver mane. "Lord, how I miss that physical presence. That 3-year-old angel. Gran'pa this, Gran'pa that. And she hardly complained. All that chemotherapy. All those needles . . ."

Wow, did I miss Jake's physical presence. His touch, his sexy, soothing voice, the oneness that bonded us. The sharing of life with my best friend, which made joys more giddy, sorrows less grueling. Now, honestly staring at denials was like fleeing from a thunderstorm into fresh sea breezes.

For one session, Monica had asked us to bring a photo of ourselves at age 6 or 7, and suggested we tell the others what the person in the picture was saying. Holding her picture up, Monica began, "This little girl is saying, 'Please like me. Can we be friends?'" Another person also confided that the child in her picture was asking for friendship. All the others indicated theirs were asking for love. I hadn't taken a picture because our albums were in storage.

"What would your little girl be saying, if you'd brought one?" Monica urged.

"She'd be saying," I grinned. "Isn't everything beautiful?"

Monica started a tape of very soft music. "This evening, we're going to go through a fantasy," she explained. "I'd like you to lie down and close your eyes." We stretched out. "Now," she coached, "take a couple of deep breaths slowly. Imagine yourself in a lovely garden. It's a beautiful day. The sun is shining, the birds are singing and everything is perfect."

On my fantasy voyage, I coasted into a formal English garden. There was a lagoon bubbling over rocks, and an umbrella of snowy orange blossoms rising from carpets of velvet grass. And whiffs of lilacs waving in the cool breezes.

Monica continued, "There's a path where you see a child coming toward you. She approaches you and asks for something. Then you ask her (or him) for something in return. Later the child leaves and you revert to your normal consciousness." Monica slightly increased the music volume.

In my reverie I surface as Mother Nature dressed in a gauzy, long, free-flowing milk-white gown. My auburn hair tinged with the sun's golden rays cascading to my shoulders, I'm perched on a filigreed marble bench with arms coupled around my knees, my feet crossed at the ankles in barely-there open sandals resting on the seat. A portrait steeped in cosmic harmony.

In the horizon, a little girl, just 6, skips into view springing down the path. Her puffed sleeved, below-the-knee full skirted alabaster organza dress, with baby blue taffeta underskirt, whirling like the sides of a circus tent in the wind.

Upon sighting the child, my frothy gown bellowing to my painted toes I float down to welcome this dynamo. And her pupils ignited with ecstasy, this child-of-nature invites me to dance with her, gripping my extended hands without breaking her beat. And together we waltz, undulating in counterclockwise circuits, our gaze locked, our hair weaving in the wind, laughing and giggling, charged with the joy of simply being alive.

Still twirling, she asks, "And what would you like me to give you?"

"What else?" I sing, "this joy of innocence, for ever and ever."

Without breaking our rhythm, she chirps "But I can't." And I know she means, You foolish thing, you know I can't do that! She then chuckles, "I have to return, you know. We have to stop."

As if to a silent countdown, I unclasp one tiny hand, then the other. Tossing me a kiss in the air, she flits away brimming with the embers of her innocence, her laughter echoing like porcelain wind chimes. I watch her figure get smaller and smaller and disappear. The English gardens once flooded with life are now only a one-dimensional painted postcard in my head.

I heard shuffling, and opened my eyes to upturned lips frozen in nostalgia.

In one of my journals, I had written:

> I'm very sorry that I've lost that innocence; that joy, that joie de vivre that I had. Everything in the world used to be beautiful—I was my loving, caring paternal, anthropomorphic God's child who went around the house singing my favorite hymn: "This is my Father's world / And to my listening ears / All nature sings and round me rings / the music of the spheres."
>
> Now no longer a dependent child, the music has changed and I must discover a richer melody.

Monica asked us to discuss our experiences. "At the age of 6 or 7 is when a child realizes whether they really do, or don't, have love," she explained. "That's why we went back to that specific period."

The other widows had asked the little girl to give them love. "In my life, specially in childhood, I never felt loved," said one. Another agreed, "I hadn't known love till I met my husband."

"This creates a double loss," Monica pressed home. "You've not only lost your husbands, but feel you've lost the singular love in your lives."

Chapter 12

Dorothy said, "On forms, I identify myself as Single, not as a Widow. Widowhood has a lot of negative connotations. When I was young, a widow lived on my street. She was pitied, and was even an outcast from the social set."

Certainly, no pity; but was disclaiming death the answer? "I feel I should acknowledge the fact that I'm now a widow," I confided.

"Why should I?" Dorothy insisted. "It's none of other peoples' business."

There was a heavy hush. "It's okay to focus on your immediate needs," Monica stressed. "Grief can't be rushed. Every person has a different agenda for grieving, and not everyone goes through the stages in the same order. And, it's always okay to use whatever support system helps."

This was the year 1981. We had all read Harold S. Kushner's *When Bad Things Happen to Good People* and agreed that the book did not address our search.

"What if you're searching for answers, and they seem just beyond reach?" Stephanie asked.

"Well, be angry if you're mad. Cry if you hurt." Monica underscored. "Sometimes you'll get answers, sometimes not. Have you thought about your dreams? Try concentrating on your dreams. A lot of times you'll get solutions, and healings, through your dreams."

At another session, Monica put us through a second visualization exercise. Lighting an island of candles in our midst, she asked us to stretch out on the floor and started a tape—guitars, like crystal waterfalls swooshing in a backdrop of piano keys. After leading us through deep breathing exercises, she instructed: "Push aside all that is cluttering your thinking. Concentrate on listening to the music. I'll guide you."

In her lilting tone she continued, "I'd like you to visualize a beautiful meadow where you are in control, serene and at one with all the beauty of nature around you. . . . You're now walking down a path toward a very special rendezvous . . ."

In my fantasy, at the end of a sinuous path I came across some steps.

"A light in the distance is becoming brighter and brighter as you approach it," Monica was saying.

I started to climb the stairs. There were ten or twelve up in one direction, then, after a threshold, more stairs in another direction. They only went up, and I kept anticipating a special something at every bend.

Monica's smooth style persevered, "You are walking toward the light. And you recognize a form in the light."

As higher and higher I climbed, way up at the summit where the mountain kisses the sky was a glow twinkling like Venus, sheathing a person. It was my Jake, poised at attention, patiently waiting for me. Like a laser beam in an ethereal spire, faster and faster I flew until I crashed into his outstretched arms.

It was like coming home. Cloaked in the radiance, we clung to each other. I could feel his head resting on mine, my cheek caressing his living, heaving chest.

Monica murmured, "You want something from the light."

What I wanted was simply to stay there. With him. And even though I knew it was an impotent wish, I held him tighter. Never, never would I let him go away again

"The person, or light, will give you something," Monica said. "A gift, that you will take with you. The person, or light, is now giving you something . . ."

Jake held up a ring: a wide, wide brilliant metal. It was round because it signified love, but it also symbolized eternity—a never-ending consciousness. And I was to take this ring back to remind me of a unity in consciousness, and eternity without end. Not a wedding ring. Much more.

"You have to leave and come back," Monica was saying.

Chapter 12

I couldn't leave. Of course, I wouldn't leave. I was staying there.

In the euphonic symmetry of guitars and piano and the absolute absence of dialogue, I knew that the others were waiting for me. Pulling my eyelids apart which felt glued, in the quavering candle-flames everything appeared unchanged. As my breathing skip-hopped in spurts, feeling like a child jerked away from a wingless flight in never-never land, I eased up.

Monica said, "Would anyone like to share your fantasy with us?" Nobody spoke. "Lisa, would you like to?"

Tears gushing down my cheeks like a broken dam, my body twitching out of control like a 5-point earthquake, I burst into spastic sobs. Soon, I felt a gentle touch on my knee, and Monica's tranquil voice, "Go ahead, Lisa. It's all right to let go."

"I'm sorry to put everyone through this," I hiccuped.

"That's what we're here for," Monica whispered. Then, "Lisa I'd like to hold you. Would that be all right?" And gathering me into her arms, Monica held me until my convulsive body was exhausted. When we pulled away, handing me a tissue Monica said, "What was it like, Lisa?"

"It was Jake," I whimpered.

"What did he say?" she urged.

I couldn't breath properly. "Nothing," I managed.

"It's okay, Lisa," Monica assured me. "What did you do?"

"We just stood there and held each other."

Monica pursued. "That was a very warm feeling wasn't it?"

A sigh escaped from the deep wells of my soul. "It was."

"It's very hard giving up that kind of love relationship, isn't it?" Monica continued.

I nodded, swallowing the lump in my throat. Afterward, with shards of ice shooting down my spine, I wept my loss all the way home. Cathartic tears.

Some weeks later we had a guest speaker—a 45-year-old school teacher with a sparkling smile who told us about losing her husband to lung cancer two years earlier. "It'll get better, believe me," she emphasized. "If you take your time and face the grief with no defenses, flowing with whatever each day may bring, the sun will shine again. Perhaps not exactly as before, but nevertheless beautifully." Waving a glittering engagement ring, she smiled, "I'm going to be married next month."

After three months in group therapy, I was ready to proceed solo. That last evening, with a firm hug, Monica affirmed, "Don't hesitate to return, if you ever feel the need." I didn't. And if I had, I would have skated back to that haven of empathy.

Jake's watch, hands stopped at 12:31, was among the personal belongings handed to Allen at the hospital. Jake wound his watch every morning, so I assumed that, like many others I'd learned of during my research, it must have been the hour his soul left his physical body. I also knew that sometimes those watches had suddenly began running again without being wound. Initially, I had placed the timepiece under my pillow, then carried it in my purse, checking often to see whether the hands had moved. When nothing happened, I set the watch on the night stand.

Two weeks later, on a Sunday evening, I noticed that the hands had advanced to 12:44. Not having witnessed the move, I assumed a jolt or jiggle must have initiated the shift, and before leaving for work the next morning noted that there was no change.

That evening, Allen and Trish were coming to have dinner with me. Allen had arrived early and fell asleep on the couch. I thought it'd be a good time to make my bed, and was reaching over to tuck the bedspread under the pillow, when I casually glanced at the watch. The hands had moved four minutes, now pointing to 12:48.

The doorbell rang. As Allen let Trish in, cupping the wristwatch in my trembling hands I walked up to them. "Mom, what is it?" Allen said examining my face.

I held out the watch. "It's changed," I said. "It had stopped at 12:44."

"Give it to me," Allen said. He shook it vigorously, and the three of us watched the second hand advance then stop in less than 30 seconds. "Are you sure you didn't shake it, Mom? It could have just run when you picked it up or shook it."

"No Allen, I didn't. It was just lying on the night stand, when I noticed it."

"Did you touch it at all?"

I shook my head. "Not until after the hands had moved." We placed the silent timepiece on the buffet table, and after they left I put the watch away in my top dresser drawer still unwound. For the next three months every time I checked, the hands pointed to 12:48.30.

On the first Saturday night in December and all day Sunday, I strongly sensed that Jake was my companion wherever I went. And he had that devilish aura, as if there was something of which he was very proud. When I went to bed I tried to figure out whether it was a special day. Whether it could be an anniversary or a commemoration of a special event. I thought I'd get some message in my dreams, but didn't. In the morning the feeling persisted. In my journal I recorded:

> He appears to be happy, which makes me happy. It's as if he's needling me to find out about something. It's like when we were going together in Africa and we used to play hide-and-seek in the apartment and he would hide in the most bizarre places. Once he hid lying flat atop one of those big, bulky African doors. The whole family joined

me in looking for him and of course we didn't see him until he jumped down giggling, very proud of himself.

On Sunday afternoon after church, I opened my dresser drawer to get into my jewelry box where I was saving a gift for a girlfriend's birthday. I noticed Jake's watch nestled in the corner tray and thought, Okay if you're here with me now make this thing run, *then* I'll know it's really you, and casually lifted the watch. The second hand was running; and instead of 12:48 the time was 12:55 and rolled into 12:56 as I held it.

Gaping at the ticking second hand I eased it on to the dresser as if it were a fragile prehistoric museum artifact that was going to disintegrate if touched. The radio was on. I turned it down and transfixed, keeping my gaze on the timepiece, dialed Allen's phone number. The line was busy. Well, I'll just call Marc in Chicago I thought, but dialed the wrong number and apologetically hung up. The watch was still running. I re-dialed and the phone rang and rang. Marc wasn't home. The watch kept ticking. Oh God, I've got to get to one of the boys. I dialed Allen a third time, it was still busy. I looked at the watch. It had run for 3 minutes. And stopped. The hands now pointed at 12:58.

I had just started a class at the Rosicrucian Society where we were introduced to the theory of 1 and 1 making 3. For example, when one man and one woman join, a new birth—a new entity—takes place. Thus three is an anointed number. Why did the watch stop after three minutes? Coincidence, or a cosmic message?

That evening, after I had convinced my skeptical mind to accept reality—that the hands of the watch had, for some reason, run automatically—I calmed my racing heart through yoga and sat with my notebook. Immediately, smoothly, the pen began to write:

Chapter 12

"The soul does not die. It just changes its cover to grow into other areas that are necessary for the evolution of the universe, working in perfect harmony with the cosmos."

In the summer, I flew out to visit Jeanne and Dennis. Jake's unwound watch was tucked in my purse and we talked about it's bizarre behavior often, and the hands continued to remain stationary. On my last Saturday I accompanied Jeanne to the grocery store, and decided to wait in the car when she went in. Casually, I removed the watch from my purse noticed it was still not running and laid it on my lap. When next I glanced at it, the second hand was ticking. Jeanne returned five minutes later and transfixed, together we watched Jake's wristwatch run another 10 minutes. Then it stopped.

Had the close bond of the four of us created a channel through which Jake's soul projected energy?

So many questions. So much mystery. As eons of life unravel uncharted paradigms, tiny bricks of knowledge will cascade into majestic clues to a unifying cosmos.

Chapter 13

Transitions

On the first anniversary of Jake's death, our families gathered to commemorate the lives of three loved ones, now freeze-framed in the month of August. I set a personal pace to tiptoe beyond the recent past and focus on the bonuses of each new day.

One Saturday, a month later, I awakened to a beep, beep like a truck's backing-up signal. This was a non-working day, and dawn was barely painting the sky. Tucking my head under a pillow I sank deeper into the covers. But the beeps drummed on and on.

I pattered to the window and sneaked a look. There were no trucks. No traffic. Not even any pedestrians. Could it be in my head? No, definitely not. Could it be from the bedroom under mine? No, not that confined. I climbed back into bed. The signals, dot-dot, followed by two fast dot-dot-dots tattooed incessantly. As I started to get drowsy I sensed a presence, much like when in a crowd one becomes aware that someone is staring at you. It was Jake lying by my side—on the left. Startled, I sprinted up to assimilate the scene closely.

It *was* Jake. Strikingly pleased and at peace. Telepathically, I screamed "It's you Jake." It was the recognition he'd been awaiting, for in the cadence of my discovery he sat up and faced me. And as I leaned very, very close to assuage my skepticism, his hypnotic gaze didn't falter: Examine me in detail, it defied, It's me! I was aware that he had a body, but didn't see it. I yearned to touch him and hug him, but my need ignited a fade-out and I pleaded, "Don't go. Jake. Please, please don't go." Like viewing in reverse a video of water spilling from a glass, the image components recollected into a focused whole. I watched the form in awe, until in the silence of my validation, it slowly evaporated.

The next morning I recalled that when Mary came to me that night in the den, it was with a message: See how great I look! Jake didn't have any message, simply a challenge to identify that it was he. Much like when he was in his physical body, more comfortable communicating silently than verbally. He looked good. Much younger, beautifully peaceful. And then, he was as suddenly gone.

Most who live in Europe are familiar with the story of Napoleon Bonaparte's appearance to his mother in Rome, on the night of his death on St. Helena in 1821. It is told that his mother, answering a knock at the door, found a man swathed in a cloak who said he was from St. Helena. As the man lifted his mantle she recognized her son, and assuming Napoleon had escaped from prison wanted to throw herself into his arms. But sidestepping her embrace, the person walked into the house and disappeared from sight.

One early dawn two years after Jake's death, I untangled myself from an overwhelming precognitive dream steeped in the death of someone close to me.

For days I speculated and meditated, in a frenzy for answers. Greg's battle with hepatitis had stabilized, and the family was confident that his former roller-coaster days were behind him. On Friday of the week of the dream, I was overpowered with the need to visit Greg. I'd never driven alone to his home thirty miles away, so called Val to see if we could go together.

"I have to stay at the office to attend a reception after work," Val said. "I'm chairing the refreshments, and there's no one who can take over. Can we go on the weekend?"

My knees began to shake. "No Val, I've got to see him tonight."

"Lisa, I don't think you can find Greg's home by yourself. Why don't you call Richard. Perhaps he can take you," she suggested.

Richard had an appointment with a client for whom he'd purchased a special rug. "Are you sure you've got to go tonight? I saw him last week, and we talked only a few days ago."

"If you can't make it, I'll find his home by myself. It shouldn't be that hard."

"Lisa, no. If you've got to see him so badly, I'll go with you. I'll reschedule my appointment," Richard offered.

We met at his oriental rugs store, left my car in his parking space and drove to Greg's home where we rang and rang the doorbell, but no-one answered. "Looks like he's not home, Lisa," Richard urged.

"Rich, he's here. We've got to get in somehow."

At the side of the property, Richard scrambled up the gated fence and helped me over. We climbed up the back stairs to an access door on the second floor. That door, too, was locked, and there was no answer to our incessant bangings. The July evening was hazing into darkness.

"Well, what shall we do?" Richard mused.

I crouched in the corner of that sliver of space, shaky elbows pressed against my knees, face cradled in my freezing fingers.

"There's something else I can try," Rich said, seizing his billfold and peeling out a credit card. With skillful maneuvering, he slid the plastic square into the side of the lock. There was a click. "Got it!" he murmured, and twisting the knob and pushing the door ajar, fumbled for the light switch.

As we stood shoulder to shoulder in the bright hallway, Greg shuffled around the corner in a loose unbelted striped cotton robe over wrinkled pajamas. Looking like an elongated caricature of his old self, his glassy gaze scouring Richard's face then mine he demanded, "Why did you come? How did you get in?"

"Why didn't you answer the door? Didn't you hear us?" Richard countered. "We've been trying to get in for half an hour."

I'd never seen Greg in a wrinkled anything. Propping himself against the wall, eyelids partially shut, he whispered. "I'm dying. And I'm not going to the hospital."

"We're here," Richard said, taking his arm and guiding him to the living room. "We're not going to take you to the hospital."

"And I don't want you calling my doctor either," Greg added. "Promise."

"Greg, have you eaten anything?" I said, slipping a pillow under his head as he eased down on the couch.

"Yes."

"What?" I lifted his legs up and covered his emaciated body with Mother's afghan.

Placing a palm on his forehead, he muttered, "I don't remember."

"Okay, we won't take you to the hospital if you will eat something," Richard bartered, motioning me toward the kitchen.

We knew there was no way we could persuade Greg into shifting to the hospital that night. While Richard heated some soup I called a hospice number in the phone book, and gave the lady who answered Greg's history and his physician's name. The next morning, persuaded by a visiting nurse, Greg was transferred to the hospital by ambulance.

Richard, Valerie and I worked out an agenda to accommodate our working hours to be with Greg at different times, and his improvement was visible.

A week later, before heading for the office, I called Greg. "He just fell asleep," the nurse said cheerfully. "He's doing better. At breakfast he was admiring the flowers his nephews sent him." Valerie was to be there from ten to noon, and Richard and I would be with him after four.

By mid-day, I couldn't concentrate on anything at work. I knew something very crucial was happening to Greg, as that foreboding dream flashed ever more consistently in the annals of my soul. As soon as my boss returned from lunch, I asked if I could leave and called Richard. "We've got to get there before four," I blurted.

"Lisa why? Have you heard anything?"

"No. I feel it's crucial that we leave now. I'm not waiting. Can you go?"

"Yes, I can go."

Clutching my car keys I said, "I'll be there in forty-five minutes."

When Richard and I rushed into Greg's room, an apron of friends standing around his propped-up body moved to create an aisle as Valerie took my arm. "The Bishop just left," she murmured. "He asked to take communion." Greg's almond-shaped eyes were curtained, his pallor only a shade more opaque than the ebbing and ascending sheets. My chest began to heave. Scurrying out I sped to an isolated hall where, bracing my quivering form against the wall, bawled.

"The doctor wants to talk to us," I heard Richard say. And he and Valerie and I, marching like recruits following a captain, entered a small lounge where, gesturing toward a tiny couch, the doctor said, "Please sit down." We crowded together on the narrow seat. Facing us on a straight-backed chair, easing forward the doctor cleared his throat. "We've all been working on . . ." He began again, "We would like Greg to get better, we've all been working on that. But . . . but, he's going the other way." He looked at each of us as if to say, You realize what I mean. We stared back. Richard's knees went into spasms. The doctor's voice droned on but I couldn't grasp what he was saying, until he stood up. "I'm very sorry," he added.

In Greg's room, with a hint of disbelief the nurse questioned, "Do you really want to stay?"

Chapter 13

I dropped into the chair by the bed and clasped Greg's weightless hand. "*I* do." I said.

"Many people don't," the nurse explained as if addressing a kindergarten group on their first school day. "It could take a long time. Most people usually go home and ask us to call them. It's not easy watching a loved one die."

I glanced at Richard hunched by the window, at Valerie gripping the iron rail. "I'm staying," I said.

Dragging the only other chair to my side, Valerie echoed, "I'm staying."

"I'm staying too," Richard nodded. "We'll all stay."

"All right," the nurse acquiesced. "You may call me any time." And left.

On the hard chair, my spine rigid as a walking stick, my knees bracing the cold metal of the bed, I cradled Greg's arm. This man, who beginning at age 10 was flooded by the enormity of eldest male responsibility in a family left behind by a dying father, now lay back at peace

Many a moment, Greg and I had collided. The first time I wore lipstick, he demanded I wipe it off and surrender the tube. I rubbed away some of the color but hid the lipstick. He saw himself as my surrogate father, my protector. I craved to be let loose, to learn from my own mistakes. Then there were times when my big brother was a pillar of support. When in high school I was studying secretarial skills, he allowed me to practice on his personal typewriter, and loaned me his shorthand dictionary, personally drilling me on brief-forms until I tested at the head of my class. His highest compliment to me was: You should have been a man—you have the brains. And although at first he had battled my plans to marry a non-Armenian, he took personal pride in introducing Jake to prurient Armenian phrases. Ultimately, his posture proud, gait unwavering, he walked me down the aisle as the arm I clung to quavered like a feather in the wind. Later, I found an envelope with a generous check tucked in my travel case.

In his sense of personal responsibility as the home provider in his father's stead, he had not married to accommodate his widowed mother and single sister. They were now gone, and the years without them had been lonely, as, like a child left all alone to fend for himself, he battled with his deteriorating health.

His chestnut hair still as luxuriant as when it whirled in the gales of the Red Sea, now it caught the sun's gleam a tad from the Golden Gate Bridge oceans away. I wanted this big brother of mine to know we were keeping vigil by his side. "Greg, if you can hear me squeeze my hand," I whispered. His fingers didn't move, but the tremor of his muscles was unmistakable. In less than a half hour, he started taking long, labored breaths. A couple of times his upper body rose.

"Greg, it's all right," I confided, caressing his arm. "It's all right, leave your body behind. You don't need it any more."

Relieved, he sank back on the pillows. He took one very prolonged breath.

I pressed the nurse's buzzer. Hard. Wouldn't let go. She came in syncopated steps, her gaze averted, and took his pulse. Not saying anything, not giving us a glance, she marched out and returned with a physician. Stationing themselves side by side opposite where I still clung to Greg, silently the doctor dragged her stethoscope up to her ears, reached down and began monitoring vital signs. Valerie grabbed my knee. Behind us, Richard hugged our shoulders. As if she were an electronic toy, the doctor stood erect releasing the stethoscope. She looked down at her watch. Turning to the nurse, in a monotone staccato she announced, "Three-twenty."

From an original nuclear family of six, it was now just Richard and me.

We recouped. Concentrating on births and weddings and new beginnings of families and friends, we skated through six summers. Then, another turn in the road. A series of strokes within a three-year period started to tear away at Richard's immune system, already weakened by diabetes. Once, when Valerie was despondent about Richard's prognosis, I started doing automatic writing to see whether Mary had any advice. Immediately, Greg came through. *"Be brave dear sister,"* my pen wrote. There it was again; only Greg warned me like that.

January rolled by with rainstorms felling giant redwoods. Rivers, claiming additional territory, dislodged homeowners along swollen banks in Northern California. But rolling hills dazzled green, and camellias nurtured buds, and cyclamens flapped crimson velvet petals to the call of the morning doves. On the second Sunday, I woke up with a pressing urgency that I see Richard. Valerie appeared calm on the phone, suggesting that I stay for dinner.

Although after his last major stroke Richard had seldom recognized me, when I walked in that afternoon, looking up with glee like a toddler who's caught sight of his first puppy, he declared, "It's my sister, Lisa. I used to take care of her when she was little. Do you remember?"

"Rich, of course I remember. I wanted to marry you when I was a little girl, but mother said I couldn't because you were my brother." Raising his shoulders to his ears and flipping his still-thick silver mane with a dash I hadn't spotted in years, he giggled.

"And remember," I prompted, "when you bought your first car—it was a black Lancia." Nodding, Richard's crinkling Clark Gable eyes sparkled with a glimpse back into his youthful abandon. "Remember, I said I could drive it, and you said go ahead, and let me sit behind the wheel. And I rolled the car off the road, then lunged to the other side, until you grabbed the brakes and we squealed to a halt."

"You kept saying you could do everything," he announced reaching for Val with nostalgic glee. "This gal always thought she could do anything, from the time she was little!"

"I'll tell you something," Val laughed. "She hasn't changed. Not one bit. She still says she can do anything—and does it. That's your sister."

Richard was having a good day. Leaning onto his companion-nurse, he strolled to the kitchen and we had a cheerful dinner hour. He even reminded his wife what pills he should be taking with his food. Buoyed by his alert demeanor, my trip home was more tranquil.

Two evenings later I was in the kitchen preparing pasta, when I heard the thud of my gate. Looking up, in the multicolored hues of footlights, I discovered Allen striding up the path. Before he had an opportunity to press the bell, I flung my front door open. "What are you doing here?" I blurted. Trish was out of town for a couple of days, and nothing stopped Allen from dashing home after work to be with their daughter, Allison.

Allen stepped in. "Mom, I have some bad news." Ashen, he stood in the foyer.

"Is it Trish? Has something happened to her?"

"No," he put an arm around my shoulder.

I searched his liquid-blue eyes mired in pain. "Allison's all right, isn't she?"

"Allison's fine Mom." He tightened his hold.

Why's he glum? It can't be Rich. Valerie said he was fine this noon, and they were getting ready for a drive. "What is it, Allen?"

"It's Uncle Richard," he said softly. "Mom, he died this afternoon."

From the kitchen, a television weatherman was profiling January snowstorms in the east. In my head a soulful strain trilled, "Turn, turn, turn . . ."

One Saturday morning, again awakened by a beep-beep, I sensed Jake's aura. Thinking it had to be in my mind, I concentrated on returning to sleep. A throbbing started at the base of my skull. My palms and soles quivered as if prodded by needles. My physical body was relaxed, my breathing was smooth and I became fully awake as outside noises faded into the horizon. Suddenly, Jake was at my side, to the right, looking exactly as he did when we first met—young, vibrant, brimming with exuberance. Cracking his roguish smile, he reached out with open palm as if to say, "Come with me, and I'll show you." It reminded me of when, hand in hand, we strolled together on the misty mountains of Eritrea in Africa. To circumvent my cultural restrictions of seeing each other only when chaperoned, I used to rise up before the sun to steal time alone together on the meandering slopes, returning before the rest of the family started their day.

Now, as he whiffed that you-don't-know-what-you're missing charm, I must have appraised him with disbelief. He signaled, "Trust me, I won't hurt you."

There's no way I can deny this is Jake, I reasoned; it should be okay. But where will he take me? "I really would love to go with you," I wavered, "but it would be terrible for the boys if I left my physical form, don't you think? It's been barely a year since they lost *you*, and I don't want them to find *me* gone also. . . No, I've got to stay with my body. I can't leave. I can't do that to our boys."

Undaunted, his spectral smile locking me in its grip, Jake kept his stance. "Trust me," he signaled. "It'll be all right."

I did so wish to learn about where he was and what it was like, though reluctant to leave my mortal cocoon. Would I have to completely abandon my physical body to go with him? And if I did, was my body healthy enough to accommodate my return? As I pondered, like a blast of fireworks, a message signaled: hold on to the Silver Cord; if you hold on, you'll be all right.

Although a moonlike luminescence engulfed us, I became aware that in order to reach where Jake wanted to take me, we would first have to travel through a dark tunnel. I wasn't prepared for that. Totally confident, Jake was at ease, as if he were simply continuing his natural life. Well, I told myself, since he's already made the transition, Jake doesn't remember how different reality is on the planet earth. Sure, I'll be okay with Jake, but I simply can't leave the boys; they'd be heartbroken—it's really too soon.

How will I handle this? When I faltered, I reverted back to the traffic noise, the poundings in the nape of my head, the sensations in my palms and soles. A dilemma.

Then I concluded, Okay, I trust Jake. He appears to have no reservations. I'll allow myself to go off with him. And I floated into a deep, deep sleep.

I woke up at seven-thirty the next morning, surprised I was still in my human form. No beeps, no poundings, no sensations. I vividly remembered my encounter with Jake, but couldn't recall any cosmic journeys.

A week later, Jake appeared again, exactly as he had before.

This time, eagerly confident, I grasp his outstretched hand which swiftly cuddles mine. He turns and begins to move as, like a trusting child on her way to a hidden adventure, I trail closely behind to a crystal, endless, bubbling stream. Stepping on a boulder, Jake spins around and beaming with his sacred secret, signals, "See? it's safe," tenderly easing me up to stand by his side. And together, fingers intertwined, as weightless as light, we leap from one boulder to the other like two 6-year-olds on a venture of discovery.

"You see?" Jake trills, "this is what it's all about. The beginning of a beautiful journey."

It is exhilarating. It is liberating. I recognize that pure, clear, shimmering stream: the essence that some call God the Father, others Universal Intelligence, or Life, or Eternity. Ethereally beautiful, safe as a womb. The evolutionary confluence to which we all eventually return.

Chapter 14

All Seasons

On the eve of what would have been Mary's 50th birthday, I found myself caught up in a bold adventure. It was a dream, where along with others, I was at a party having a fantastic time. The festivities were an ongoing activity, but like a player in a drama it appeared to be time for me to exit. A flawless, sleek, snow-white, elongated vehicle came into view from behind me with Mary at the wheel, easing into a full stop directly at my feet. Completely taken aback, I leaned over and peered in to make certain the driver was really Mary. It was.

"How come you're driving?" I asked. "Mary, you don't know how to drive."

Tossing me a smile, she motioned, "Get in."

I studied the scenario. The motor was purring like a private limo ready to take off as soon as I stepped in. No way, I'm not getting in this thing, I calculated. I don't want to go with Mary: she's dead.

Without breaking her smile, Mary signaled, "Come in, I'll take you to the next level where you're headed."

Gripping the open window I stuck my head partially in and assessed the inside of the vehicle. Aside from Mary, it was empty. I dragged my fingers to the outside and straightening up declared, "No. I don't want to go. I'm having too much fun here."

For a couple of seconds, unblinking, Mary looked me over the way a parent appraises a child's tenacity, then acquiesced, "All right. I'll come back for you in a year." I stepped back and watched the car's smooth retreat into a distant horizon.

Chapter 14

The next day, every detail of the dream haunted me. Exactly what did coming back in a year mean? Wasn't time on our planet separate from those who've made their transition? Or was the dream an alert of a danger?

Three days later, at the end of the workday a colleague and I joined a friend who had just returned from a European vacation, for cocktails. It was a carefree, exciting evening with gales of laughter at tales of Italian machos who consider a pinch on the buttock a complementary gesture to female tourists. It was about seven forty-five when, with the setting sun forcing me to strain for clear vision spots ahead, I approached the turnoff to my townhouse complex

Easing into the left-turn curve, I noticed the security guard standing by the open gate. I stopped, dropped the remote back into the door pocket, and not seeing or hearing any approaching traffic, turned my wheels onto the complex approach.

Suddenly blanketed in a titanic explosion, my vehicle began to rotate counter-clockwise as syncopated echoes of the eruption vibrated in my head. Then my car came to an abrupt stop. When my senses balanced, I noticed that instead of heading into the complex I was now jutting out into the oncoming traffic. And the motor was still running. Maybe I should turn this thing off, I thought, it's not going anywhere. I turned the key and the motor died.

Through the millions of cracks of my windshield, the sun's glare twinkled here and there. All of the car windows were blown out. My briefcase and handbag, which were on the seat next to me, were now bunched up on the floor. The rear right of the vehicle was completely smashed in. It felt as if I were sitting on the road rather than in my car. With my hands still on the steering wheel, I couldn't move. The driver's door creaked ajar, and I heard a male voice, "Are you all right?"

Startled, I spotted a head inches from mine and only then realized I'd been in a car accident. "I'm all right," I heard a raspy echo sounding like my voice.

"Can you move?" the stranger urged. When he reached over to unbuckle my seat belt, I discovered that the inside of the car was flooded with glass crystals. "Here, I'll help you," the man said, kicking the door back as he eased me out. "Can you stand up?" He was holding my left hand and my wrist hurt a little.

"I'm fine," I whimpered, balancing on wobbly knees like a newborn doe.

There were people all around. My demolished car with no windows, sat on bare wheels. There was a steel gray double-truck parked at an angle, on the other side of the road. A frightened young man in a black sports-cap sauntered over and identified himself as the driver of the truck. "You turned right in front of me," he said clearing his throat. "Didn't you see me?"

I shook my head. "I didn't see you. The sun was in my eyes."

The police came and began taking measurements. The fire engine arrived and began to hose down the area. There was activity everywhere and people in groups on the grass talking to each other. "Your vehicle is totaled," a policeman said. "Are you sure you don't need to be checked? I think you should. We can take you out to the hospital."

"No thank you," I said. "I'm all right. My wrist just hurts a little."

I could walk. I could think. A neighbor helped me call Allen and Trish who rushed over and drove me to the hospital for observation. With only a sprained wrist, I was released and returned home before eleven. My annihilated car had been towed away.

How did I escape? And, did I have only one earth-year left?

Some time later, one evening I took pen in hand and asked Mary to explain her parting message "I'll be back in a year."

"Remember your not wanting to come with me? You must want to come here," the writing said.

"Does that mean that I'll still have a choice?"

"Yes," was the fast answer.

Another time I was doing automatic writing when Greg came through. He said it was Mary who had protected me from being killed in the accident. I remind myself that a year on earth is not the same time-frame as a year in the cosmos. And perhaps in some cases we are given a choice.

One night in a vivid dream I found myself swimming in an ocean through gargantuan hazards: waves and wind and turbulence, even black, granite-like rocks. But I was intent on trying to reach Jake standing with some people on the other side calmly waiting for me. He's dead, I told myself, how can he be waiting for me out there. How can I stay alive in these waters when I've never learned how to swim, floating as if it's simply oxygen.

Later, as I took pen in hand to see if I could still communicate, before writing my question "Was that really you waiting for me on the other side of the turbulent waters in my dream?" the words automatically formed on paper.

> *"Yes that night I was with you. . . . We are helping you to grow in understanding.*
> (By now I took it for granted that those who've made their transition work with others.) *We'll always show you how to understand love, and God will lead the way."*

No, not God, I thought. I don't believe in a personal God any more. My innocence has disappeared. All my joy in a personal, protective God has now dissolved into the reality of a universal, impersonal cosmos. Before I had a chance to write down my thoughts, the pen moved:

> *"Yes I know you don't believe in God like you did before, but God is with you showing you the way. It is not a personal God but a universal intelligence. . . There is consciousness everywhere. On other planets, in different ways . . . The planet earth is just a small segment of the answer. We must go on to better things . . .*
>
> *"I was able to learn my lessons very fast. We never lose our life but we, you and I, just change bodies. . . . I want you to continue to love me, but also know that we're moving on at different levels."*

Healing from loss is a constant, ongoing effort of concentrating on the now, building on all the yesterdays. And laughter can initiate a soothing balm on the highway of recovery, which I embraced with the help of long-time close friends, Shirley and Megan Kashnan without whom my own rally would have been at a snail's pace. Many a Saturday evening they insisted I join them for dinner, and together we fed on each others' silliness. Their house-bound mother was deteriorating from a chronic long illness, and we discovered utilizing the sunshine of laughter purged our fears and made the upcoming week a little easier to face.

I smile at an incident the day before Mother's wake. On that sizzling August afternoon in San Francisco, Val and Grace and I were sitting in Greg's steamy kitchen sipping coffee, when I glanced up to discover a window above the sink, closed. Hoping to encourage some kind of a breeze I sprang up and pushed a panel partly open, getting it crookedly stuck half way.

Rising from her chair Valerie warned, "Lisa, stop. Mama said that window was intentionally closed shut because they could never get it to work right." She sighed. "Your brother's going to be furious."

What to do! We found a ladder in the basement and while Grace held it steady, I (the tallest), climbed to the top. Couldn't even touch the bottom of the frame. Just then a neighbor's college-age son came out of his home and was walking to his car on the street when I twisted around. "Sir," I yelled, "could you please do us a favor? My mother died yesterday, and without knowing we shouldn't, I opened this window. It's now stuck. And we just can't get it back closed. We didn't know we weren't supposed to open it."

"Sure," he said, assessing the situation. And while Grace and I held the ladder he manipulated the panel shut.

When we went inside Grace said, "Aunty, that was using your feminine wiles."

"Yes it was, wasn't it?" I giggled. "It worked, didn't it?" And the three of us went into bursts of laughter. It was the escape we needed in the midst of a very sad, solemn afternoon.

Research has indicated that a sense of humor contributes greatly to a person's mental health and laughter reduces stress, minimizes pain and even enhances the immune system. Some physical education professionals believe that laughter is healthy for muscles, providing an aerobic workout. Lowering blood pressure and heart rate, laughter causes the body to release adrenaline and endorphins—natural pain killers.

Psychologists agree that laughter's significant therapy is the release of tension, which author Norman Cousins referred to as the "panic blocker," making it easier to feel more in control. The more gloomy one feels, the more important a role laughter plays in our consciousness—specially laughter with family and friends.

Once, after a visit, I was driving Marc to the airport when he said. "Mom, Dad had such a resiliency about him. I wish he'd taken the time to write down some of the understanding and knowledge which made him so strong in coping with adversity. He must've had a tremendous secret. I could never have done half as well as Dad during the last five years."

A letter from a close friend outlined how, when helping his mother to recall Jake, "as soon as she saw the first picture, she remembered all the tricks he used to play on her." I said, "You know Marc, I'm not sure whether it's inborn, or whether it's developed. There was one thing about your dad. He never lost his sense of humor. Once, when he returned from an interview I asked him how it went. 'I diapered him,' he announced."

On my way home from the airport, I thought of an incident in the Buffalo area where I had started selling real estate. Having just made my first sale, I was titillating the details of my success. "You should have seen it tonight. Everything was perfect. The street was sooo well lit, it looked beautiful. Well-l lighted . . . Well lit. What is it Jake? Lit or lighted?"

With a devilish smile that began at the corners of his lips and brimmed to the depths of his eyes like the full moon dancing on the Nile, he calmly said, "I know! Illuminated."

Cherishing our yesterdays, freeing the past to celebrate todays, I moved out of the apartment into a townhouse in the Silicon Valley. As the calendar flipped, I waded into the dating game of singles parties, video hook-ups, even personal ads and blind dates. When I wasn't looking, I discovered that my adrenaline did light up my spine and my breath hop-scotch at a certain voice on the telephone. To be in love and bask in that reflection is a rare blessing. But sometimes, as in my case, when the pieces of the puzzle don't fit correctly, one decides to travel solo.

Chapter 14

Losses are inherent in the very nature of the cosmos often balanced with the wonder, awe and joy of a new birth. Marc brought a new member into the family—Marcia—for whom he'd been searching for a long time. And life began giving us special sunshine hours as I, like other grandparents, discovered the tenacity of universal life through the miracle of the birth of a new baby in the family, first with Marcia and Marc's son. Now, I'm blessed with five of those miracles, three boys and two girls.

Because Jake and I had only boys, the addition of girls to our family was particularly exciting to me. And I met both granddaughters before their birth.

Trish was two weeks past her due date, when in that zone between sleep and wakefulness, I found myself cloaked in the timeless, spaceless aura of universality. The atmosphere, a suspended palette of misty blues and lilacs and pale pinks much like dusk in the horizon of an ocean, was peaceful and familiar. I watched in awe as the contour of a Homo sapiens baby wafted toward me, her piercing blue eyes bonding with the depths of my soul, her chubby alabaster-sheen face glowing as she floated closer and closer, nestled in a mantle of a nurturing ethereal cornucopia. And I knew, this was Allen's daughter that Trish was carrying.

"There you are," I exclaimed, thinking that all I had to do was stretch out my arms for her to swoosh into. "Alive and radiant. So healthy, so beautiful. Ready to be born."

"Not yet," she fluttered, content in her habitat.

"You're not?" I wavered. "Well, you're going to get so big before you're born. Just like your dad. He was three weeks overdue."

"Aha," she giggled. "So will I."

A week later, as I cuddled my almost 9 lb. granddaughter just hours after she was born, our gaze locked again. I know, I smiled through the curtain of tears clouding my vision, we've already met.

Some years later, Marc and Marcia were expecting their third child when, soon after my arrival in Chicago to spend Thanksgiving together, I began to feel that Mary was following me. Everywhere. Once, I even stopped at the bottom of the stairs and peered around suspiciously before entering the kitchen. No, there were no visible abnormalities. Everything appeared normal. The next morning I was walking downstairs for breakfast when I heard echoes of Mary's hearty, earthy laugh. Okay Sis, I thought, you're here and I acknowledge you. You're happy about something. You'd like me to know it too. But what?

Before I reached the bottom of the stairs I heard Mary's signal, "It's a girl. There's going to be a daughter in Marc and Marcia's family." And, for the rest of my stay, Mary's presence was interwoven with a vision of a blue-eyed, gleeful, outgoing, hearty baby girl, lively with the energies of life on the planet earth.

As they awaited amnio test results, Marc and Marcia, already parents of two boys, now daydreamed of a daughter. And, respecting their privacy and the joys of their own discovery, I didn't share what I knew. Back home one evening I got a call. "Mom," Marc's beaming voice riffled across the wires. "Would you like to know what your next grandchild is going to be?"

"I already know," I chuckled.

"You do? Well, what is it?" he challenged.

"It's a girl," I sang, "Congratulations."

"It certainly is," Marc said, adding to his wife on the other line, "I told you Mom would know."

Chapter 14

And when I went back to meet Tyler, she examined me with those electrifying blue eyes and nestled close to my soul. I knew that Mary stood nearby glowing with joy.

A time to build. . . . A time to be born.

Throughout recorded human history there has been a persistent popular belief that some people possess a power of gathering knowledge other than through scientifically proven sensory faculties. From Cassandra in Greek mythology, to Biblical prophets such as Isaiah in the Bible to Swedenborg in the 19th century to present day genuine clairvoyants, the past and future have at times materialized with no peripheries.

One recent evening at the theater, while waiting for the movie to begin, a friend and I were discussing one of my psychic experiences in low tones when I saw a hand grip the back of the seat in front of us and, in a frenzy, the fingers reach out for something or someone. Then the person in the seat turned around and stretched her hand out. I didn't recognize the woman, but realizing she was groping for me, clasped her stiff fingers.

Breathlessly, she whispered, "I need a healing."

"Excuse me?" I asked, leaning closer.

"You're psychic. I need a psychic healing," she confided.

Her hand was burning with fever. Her dark curls were clinging to parts of her forehead. Gently touching her shoulder I whispered, "I'm sorry, I don't do healings. Are you all right?"

"I'm homeless. I lost my job. I live in my car," she said in a raspy voice.

My heart sank. She was wearing a quality wool coat. Looked clean and alert.

"Can't you live in a shelter?" I suggested.

She clung to my hand. "No, no. I don't want to. I prefer living in my car. When I was married, I lived in my own home up on the hill."

We were in a four-plex movie theater where for a $2.00 biannual membership fee one could get in for $2.00. It was cold and rainy outside. "I come here and when it closes, I get in my car," she continued. "I'm so sick right now. I've got to get healed."

The lights began to dim. "I'm sorry. I really don't do healings," I said squeezing her hand as I released it.

When I scooted back up on my seat, my friend turned to me, "Are you all right?"

"I'll be all right."

As soon as the movie was over, the woman rushed out. Wanting to give her some money, we searched the crowd, but she'd disappeared. Probably gone into another theater to keep warm. For a long time I thought of that woman desperately seeking a supernatural physical healing through a psychic.

On the other extreme are others, like, for example, advice columnist Ann Landers. Answering a reader's request of whether a clairvoyant friend could develop her psychic abilities to "receive" only good news, Landers wrote: "I don't believe certain people can accurately predict catastrophes. The best they can do is guess." She suggested that the friend in question "get counseling to deal with her anxieties about what she perceives as her 'gift.'"

These two incidents highlight extremes of how a psychic person is perceived: either as a miracle worker or one in need of psychiatric help. There are those in the middle who've had glimpses of precognition (beyond hunches) which they're not interested in pursuing, and a group who want to enhance whatever this extra sensory perception may be.

Chapter 14

My thirst for understanding universal consciousness began even before my teens. I recall stretching out on the lush grass where the White and Blue Nile merge to pursue their odyssey to the Mediterranean, peering at the azure skies twinkling through the leaves and branches of balsam trees, and wondering how long and far I'd have to fly to meld with the energies of the vast universe. I never tired of eavesdropping on chirping sparrows, or studying crocodiles at play, as I wondered about their self image, their family connections, their bond to the universe could be. Nights, when we'd lie on our outdoor beds, I'd study the brilliant twinkling stars against their black backdrop and know there was a depth and a bond between Man and all of the universe. So much to learn! For every thinking person's probe into reality is an ongoing journey.

And what is the final reward? An acknowledgment that life is in the living and savoring of every minute as we sometimes stagger, sometimes fly without wings, in the spiraling evolution of an all-encompassing consciousness.

EPILOGUE

The Quest

As science, cosmotology, physics, neurology, psychology, philosophy, religion, and spirituality, band together to seek answers to the nature of consciousness, a true child of the cosmos is on a quest for growth, perception and balance.

Creation

Every ancient civilization—Egyptian, Chinese, Hindu, Judaic, Greek, Roman—had its own story of creation, recited only in the narrow confines of religion. The theory of the Big Bang—that the universe came into being in one single violent explosion where every atom in our stars, galaxies, people, plants were breathed into being from the original source—has become acceptable by most scientists. Many religious leaders, including Pope John Paul II, believe that the Big Bang, in theory, is compatible with divine creation. Fundamentalist Jews, Christians and others who interpret the Scriptures literally, believe that God created the earth in six 24-hour days and "rested" on the seventh: Period.

Whether one believes that "God" created life in six days or with an instant Big Bang, all life is an offspring of an original seed in an evolutionary expansion. And most agree that all living matter functions within universal laws.

Reincarnation

Nearly all the world's people conform to the religion into which they are born. Some believe that life on the planet Earth is a one-time experience, others that it is a series of repeat incarnations.

While belief in reincarnation is most characteristic of Eastern religions, it was a very prominent philosophy of prehistoric religions and ancient Greeks and Egyptians, and was a prevalent part of the age in which Christianity began. Plato was an avid believer in reincarnation. The state of consciousness between incarnations, going back to the original *Tibetan Book of the Dead,* is referred to as the *bardo,* where each soul dwells in an existence formulated from lessons learned, in a universe devoid of time or space.

Orthodox Christianity, Islam and Judaism, disavow the theory of reincarnation: in its original interpretation, the principle of rebirth of the soul in successive existences of human, animal, or vegetable form on a journey of eventual release from the cycle of birth and death into pure enlightenment.

In the Western world, reincarnation is generally accepted as the theory of a succession of Homo sapiens births. It became prominent in the 1950s, when a woman named "Bridey Murphy" assumed to recollect, under hypnosis, that in 1864 she had died from a fall down a flight of stairs in Ireland. Murphy, then a 27-year-old mother whose real name was Ginny Tighe, as a child had lived in Chicago across the street from a woman named Bridey. When the story broke, Tighe refused to be identified, and never attempted to profit from the enormous publicity.

The theory was again headlined in 1996 when a 4-year-old American born in Seattle was turned over by his mother to

Buddhist monks in Katmandu, Nepal, who hailed the boy as the reincarnation of the Dalai Lama.

Some therapists who help subjects regress to previous lives present the theory of group reincarnation, where members of families are reborn into the same family unit to work out previous unresolved conflicts. This, labeled *karma*, is the theory of Cause and Effect in the soul's evolutionary progression.

Whether a soul is reincarnated in successive cycles, or whether, as the saying goes, "one lives only once," life on the planet earth is ventured one at a time. Thus, for many on the quest, the ability to concentrate and learn from the process of living each day in its maximum parameter, is more significant than the determination of whether one has lived before.

Euthanasia

On the other end of the theory of having to suffer because of a karmic cause in a previous incarnation, in the Western world there accelerated in the 1990s a humanitarian emphasis on euthanasia (from the Greek, painless, happy death), and death and dying began to come out of the closet. In the mid-90s, an eight-year survey in the United States, funded by the Robert Wood Johnson Foundation, reported that, in a culture that views death as a defeat, most doctors ignore patients' wishes to die in dignity. On the other hand, some who have watched a family member suffer, even while grieving their loss, look at euthanasia not as assisted suicide but as easing a loved one into a painless peace.

In 1994, Oregon became the first state to pass a law allowing physician-assisted suicide, which a federal judge immediately ruled unconstitutional. Three years later the vote was reaffirmed and opponents again mobilized to continue their fight, even as polls in the United States indicated that most Americans want the option of determining their own right to a peaceful exit. After five months of uncertainty, in March 1998 a grandmother in her 80s suffering from breast cancer was publicly acknowledged as the first person to use the state's doctor-assisted suicide law.

Battling prostate cancer, former French President François Mitterrand had spent much of his last year reading literature about death and questioning experts on the subject. Paris newspapers reported that, after learning from his doctor he would last only three days if he were to drop all medication but his pain killers, Mitterrand suspended therapy. He delivered handwritten instructions for his funeral, then concluded his 800-page memoirs. Two days later, in January 1996, Mitterrand died at age 79.

The revered prolific master novelist James A. Michener (best loved for his 1947 Pulitzer Prize winner *Tales of the South Pacific,* later spun into a musical) was a passionate lobbyist of the right to die. Michener continued to work close to home until in 1997, at the age of 90, he commanded his doctors to halt life-sustaining kidney dialysis treatments. He died a few days later.

In 1997, it was reported that 2.4 percent of deaths in the Netherlands—where doctors are allowed to discuss the ending of life with suffering patients—occurred with a doctor's assistance.

Dr. Jack Kevorkian, the controversial Michigan retired pathologist, who in 1990 openly began doctor-assisted suicides in the United States, has now become a global euphemism for euthanasia. Some label Kevorkian an opportunist; others think of him as "the tender mercies doctor," sincerely dedicated to aiding terminally ill patients who wish to make their transitions in dignity. Unveiling guidelines for regulated physician-assisted suicide, Dr. Kevorkian introduced a new medical specialty, an "obitiatrist," who, working independently and with no professional fees, would relieve the patient's personal physician of making the final decision.

Although loving hospice care is thought to be accessible to most terminal patients in developed countries, the right-to-die will continue to be an emotionally charged controversy because it is based on religious beliefs. Those who insist that doctors should not assist in the process of physical death quote the Oath of Hippocrates (thought to have originated from a Greek physician in 300 B.C., which in its original form prohibited participation in surgery and abortion). Others who have watched loved ones lose their dignity and suffer in agony, ask: Why is it humanitarian to end the suffering of animals and not human beings? They insist that those asking for the end of their turmoil want autonomy, the right to make decisions on their own medical care, the right to be free of unwanted pain in the face of no foreseen recovery and imminent death.

When at one time the medical profession appeared to be focused on keeping everyone alive at all costs, industrialized cultures are beginning to consider the ethics and wisdom and compassion for the quality of life. In the 90s there also began an overwhelming increase in the number of ethicists (the United States in 1997 had more than 700), whose primary responsibility is not to police the medical profession but to facilitate looking at options.

A Berkeley, California, based firm, Bioethics Consultation Group Inc., founded in 1985 and headed by Dr. John Golenski, a medical ethicist, has helped train ethics committees of more than 200 hospitals and revamped Oregon's Medicaid system. Golenski, a former Jesuit priest who watched his mother die from what was originally diagnosed as breast cancer, believes that the human species' ethical choices will not simply be about death and dying, but about the quality of life.

Those who have faced death often agree, that it is only when we acknowledge the inevitability of death do we renew our zest for quality of life.

The Life Cycle

The challenge for those seeking answers is why it appears that sometimes miracles happen and other times they don't. As we mature, one of the most essential principles we embrace is that life goes through adjustments, changes, and, in turn, all seasons. In what Man perceives as the normal process, a seed becomes a new life, a baby becomes a child, a child grows into adulthood and an adult evolves into a physically old person which in turn we must release into physical death.

But life on this planet doesn't always follow what we consider nature's natural progression. Of course babies die, and children do not always grow into adulthood, and many do not reach old age. And even if they do, there is so much suffering. Why?

Therein is the question that religions have been battling. Is there a purpose for suffering, for the dying of infants before having a chance to live, leaving behind grieving parents who are never the same for the rest of their lives?

Some, like me, believe that there is no *one* pat answer. There are many causes for pain and suffering due to multiple combinations of variables, circumstances and reasons in everything that happens. At times a soul may volunteer to serve as a "sacrifice," for a greater good. A good example on the human level was the loss of our space shuttle Challenger in January, 1986. Although those who gave their lives did not consciously do so, they took the risk voluntarily to further the cause of space travel. And out of their negative loss, many family members have become active in positive programs encouraging young people to pursue careers in space and science.

I believe that in the process of life on the planet Earth some diseases are not curable, some chaos exists in the midst of order and there are no blanket solutions. Many factors go into the composition of the outcome of why a certain process occurs. Sometimes a person escapes death through sheer will, or a "miracle." Sometimes not. And, at this time in the evolution of the human species, we simply don't know all the answers except that in the animal kingdom the law demonstrates survival of the fittest.

This, the beginning of a new millennium, is an exciting period for the expansion of consciousness. In the United States, innovative pain control, meditation and stress reduction clinics through Yoga and similar techniques associated with hospitals is growing. It is now generally accepted in the medical field that prayer and/or meditation have shown to lower heart rate, breathing rate and brain-wave activity. There is a stimulating emphasis on spirituality more than religiosity.

In North America, with the resurgence of a search for spiritual meaning, quick-fix answers, sleight-of-hand healings and shamanism has grown into a billion-dollar industry making it tough for the true seeker to separate the authentic from the bogus.

Genuine, responsible psychics are those who are on a continuous quest for answers to the nature of consciousness—a consciousness of not only the human species, but of all forms of visible and invisible interdependent life in an evolutionary cosmos, functioning within principles actuated by ever-changing variables.

The Psi Factors

All extrasensory experiences—visions, prophetic dreams, mental telepathy—occur because of a change in that person's state of consciousness (referred to as the norm), transcending presently accepted theories of time, space and environment. This exposure, or ability, as yet has no better label than a psychic or paranormal experience. Psychic, from the Greek, *psychikos* meaning "of the soul, spiritual," presently reflecting phenomena outside or beyond the range of what is considered normal.

The psi researcher is interested not in dreams where suppressed wishes materialize to allow the working-through of unconscious wishes, but states of consciousness that are followed by a waking event connected to the experience.

What are the factors that enhance psi capacity?

In addition to individual natural aptitude and proficiency, so many changing variables impact consciousness. The most important factor in enhancing sensitivities is to pay attention and accept with an open mind extra sensory feelings or visuals. Especially when precognitive messages occur while in the dream state, it is important to acknowledge being ready to receive the message. Stay still if it is possible. Don't move. Pay attention to your body, your mind and all variables in your environment.

Interpretation

All exchange of information, unless specifically fine-tuned, is inherently subject to misinterpretation. The Homo sapiens' extent and precision of communication has been limited by the degree in which he shares in common words and associations through recognized sensory media. Our present, most common accepted form of communication—speech—is the process of making noises through our voice-box, and hearing it through our ears, then gleaning the meaning of the word. Another accepted mode of communication is that of writing, gesturing with the fingers, or, for the blind, the Braille code. Those who speak several languages know that it is not always possible to transfer a specific meaning into an exact interpretation. For its thrust and flavor, one must often learn the language and sometimes symbolism unique to that language. Even reading and understanding the written word requires a series of definitions and clarifications: one appraises a group of characters, transposes the group into a word, which then needs to be deciphered into its exact meaning. Art, for instance, may be one person's garbage or another's haven. Or dance, which becomes meaningful through the interpretation of a multiple of communication forms: body, movement, space, music. I believe that with each generation, forms of communication between all species will advance through natural evolutionary progression, fine-tuning what at one time was the only form of communication—telepathy.

Communication

Many in Asia believe in a fundamental life force termed *"ki"* utilized to improve energy, health and performance. Sony Corporation in Japan in the 1990s set up a laboratory called "ESPER" (Extra-Sensory Perception and Excitation Research), for experimentation in their goal for shared identifiable elements of telepathy and *ki*. In Japan, a Ministry of International Trade and Industry foundation, has also set up a committee to look at *ki*.

The simple ESP cards began by Dr. J. B. Rhine and associates in a small lab in the Duke University Psychology Department has escalated to sophisticated electronic techniques worldwide by dedicated parapsychologists. In the mid 1990s there began a series of mental telepathy experiments in four independent "Ganzfeld chambers" at various locations worldwide. Ganzfeld experiments place a sender and receiver (strangers to each other) in separate soundproof rooms where the receiver attempts to tune in to pictures that the sender views on a repeated video image. It has been observed that those who perform well in the experiments tend to share certain common traits: 1) those who have already had some kind of paranormal experience, 2) those who have learned to still the mind through meditation techniques or hypnosis and 3) those who are in the artistic, musical or other creative fields.

Other parapsychological experiments have shown high scorers to be those who believe in a "sixth sense," and those who are of a cheerful, happy nature with an openness to others, who easily lower barriers between groups. A generally cheerful, friendly, informal experimentation atmosphere also appears to favor the positive operation of psychic experience

In controlled lab experiments, the following has also shown to promote more positive ESP results:

First:
Relaxation. The development of a stillness; a state in which the mind is not active with thoughts and images.

Second:
Motivation. There is a relationship between the degree a person wants to achieve success and actual results. This explains mental telepathy between people who are emotionally close.

Third:
A dissociation, or a "splitting" of the mind, or a realization of a higher consciousness—an intensification in the individual's state of consciousness.

A great number of primitive people, like those in Africa and the Maori in Australia—whose focus is on family unity and group protection unencumbered by reliance on technology, whose identification with nature and a universe where physical death is part of life—seem to inhabit a natural psychic world intuitively aware of imminent danger or death. I have found that those cultures which accept a knowing not explained through our accepted senses, and beginning in childhood promote and encourage the openness of discussion about prophetic dreams, appear to develop it naturally. In the Armenian culture, for example, it is not unusual for the family group to discuss a dream of the previous night at breakfast expecting an interpretation of its symbolic message.

Very early in life, close-knit families realize that a "sixth sense" is not hampered by distance. After I married and moved from Africa to the United States, there was a deep meaningful non-verbal communication between me and my family. Mother always knew when there were distinct events in my life—whether they were joyous or difficult.

<u>Soil and Soul</u>

Belief in super-conscious psychic communication is more prevalent in those who consider themselves spiritual rather than religious; an altruism that encompasses all living forms in the universe focusing on an all-encompassing cosmos, where all laws—natural, scientific and spiritual—meld into a "sixth sense."

Like psychologist Carl Jung, who suggested that the land one comes from is reflected in one's soul, I've found that environment and geographical locations are strong components in soul sensitivity. And it is exhilarating when we have moments of genuine reality.

This was emphasized to me when Trish and I were on an Amazon trip. One day, our group was transported by two motorized canoes to a tributary in a remote location. The humidity was so high, that what appeared like rocks disintegrated into pulverized elements even as we watched. At one point, our guides turned off the electric motors and let our canoes meander. As we drifted on those waters that had no beginning and no end, suddenly an unparalleled silence permeated our space, in the purity of that hypnotic hush transforming all into a reverence of universality.

On my first visit to Delphi in Greece, I was overpowered with a suffusion of cosmic unity totally unanticipated. It was as if I'd spent a night alone on the highest mountain on earth, mantled in a seductive sixth dimension of energies fusing the present, the past, and the future.

I recalled the story of King Croesus of Lydia who was said to have sought an oracle from Delphi, on whether to go to war with Persia. Informed by the priestess that "such a war would overthrow the strength of an empire," Croesus attacked. He was, of course, defeated and captured. An empire did fall. But it was the empire of the King, not that of Persia that fell, making it very clear that the deciphering of universal awareness is extremely complicated and often not clear until the event occurs.

The Vedas are saturated with identification of soil and soul. For cultures such as some American Indians, African tribes, Hasidic Jews, communities gather in reverence at mid-harvest to celebrate not only the earth's bounties but also to allow the spirit of soil and soul to co-exist in mutual peace.

Much like these sacred reveries for the ground, plants and animals, a spiritual person has a deep sensitivity to all things on the planet Earth, recognizing that each projected form of energy is a segment of an omniscient whole. And, in this enhanced consciousness of synthesis, naturally "tunes in" to wave lengths emanating from man, nature and the Cosmos.

A spiritual person finds God in peace and tranquillity. A spiritual person hears the melody of the cosmos in a bird's chirp, the rhythm of a baby's breath. A spiritual person marvels at the cadence of the ocean waves, the reflection of the sun on the grass, and the dew on a bud.

A spiritual person tuned to the cosmos meditates rather than prays. I like the adage: Prayer is talking to God; Meditation is listening to God.

In the Judeo-Islamic-Christian discipline, the word *meditation* goes back to Genesis where Isaac was reported to have gone out to meditate in the field. The Psalms have several references to meditation, and there is at least one instance in the New Testament, where in the Revised Standard Version, Jesus uses the word.

When people tell me they'd like to learn to meditate, what I've found they really want to learn to do, is to control their thinking so that they may be able to concentrate on a given end result.

Back in the 1960s, a rush of gurus and meditation techniques each claimed to unleash magical abilities. Transcendental Meditation, calling itself the "Science of Creative Intelligence" teaches the philosophy that every thing or person in the universe has its own unique vibration. A TM student is given his or her unique secret sound, a "mantra" (a chant), which, when sounded out, helps reposition that person or entity in its rightful universal place. The mantra, repeated over and over again becomes the focal magnet to prevent the mind from wondering. Although the mantra vibrations are considered to be universal, the meanings of the chants are in Sanskrit, the language of the original proponents of the method. At a meeting in Boston in 1995, medical experts interested in the field agreed that isolating the mind from external destruction and focusing on the repetition of anything internally meaningful to the patient (whether it be prayer, meditation or simply OOMM), has shown to introduce relaxation and induce healing in stress-related diseases.

Each person approaches meditation with a basic need. Some seek peace of mind. Some strive for healing of body. Some reach for inspiration. Some, to become a channel for good. Others meditate to transcend time and space into a universal consciousness, where the Little Man is illuminated by, or makes contact with, the Big Infinite or God.

Practiced alone, for the serious seeker it is wise to put aside a specific time in a special quiet place, daily, to allow the experience to recharge one's batteries. Some fashion this niche by rising earlier than the rest of the family, identifying with the renewal of the sun's rays with a renewal of their own depth. Some are able to take this time after other members of the family have left for the day, initiating their own day with a productivity filtered from being still and knowing that all things are one. Some devote a few minutes in the middle of their workday, only withdrawing momentarily from a hectic schedule by closing their eyes and utilizing deep breathing techniques, perhaps repeating a meaningful phrase. Mine has often been "I let go and let peace."

Meditation before bedtime has been found to be very profitable by those who suffer from insomnia. And, especially at bedtime, a ritualistic remembrance of all the good that has been a part of that day becomes very comforting. Some find that even if they cannot recall a specific positive experience, they can concentrate on something that could have been traumatic if different. For example, a safe drive to a destination without a car accident.

These forms of discipline must be approached with dedication to allow results to develop through repeated practice, practice and practice. For stilling the mind and focusing on a positive outcome minimizes fear and panic, in turn energizing the physical body to function without the added stress of anxiety.

Cosmic Consciousness

I believe that what is now referred to as "psychic ability" will some day be a very normal, accepted sensory perception for Homo sapiens, and anthropologists will label our present non-acceptance of cosmic awareness as the primitive ages. Having been fortunate enough to have been exposed to cultures where even a voice on the telephone zaps like miracles from the sky, I know that what seems a miracle today will be tomorrow's everyday technology.

Over a half century ago, psychologist Dr. Richard M. Bucke coined the phrase *Cosmic Consciousness.* Dr. Bucke believed that in the evolution of the human species, a new ability first begins to appear in a small number of people, then expands in a very orderly, evolutionary development process. As an example, Dr. Bucke offered Man's discernment of various colors as a faculty developed only a few thousands of years ago. (There were no names of colors in primitive Indo-European or Sanskrit root words.) It is believed that fifteen or twenty thousand years ago Man saw everything in only one tint, first distinguishing red and black, later red, yellow and black, still later adding white. Some suggest that the faculty of perceiving different fragrances is also recently acquired.

Epilogue

For the past hundred years, prominent scientists have been attempting to understand the scientific functions of the brain and the power of the mind. A high majority have concluded that the brain, in addition to being both a chemical and electrical complex, is governed by a mystical spiritual energy that permeates all existence.

Scientists now know that there are specific areas in the brain which perform identifiable functions. In a series of documentaries entitled *Human Behavior* shown on public television in the early 1980s, there was a case history of a woman whose brain was accidentally stimulated during surgery giving her the ability to hear music when there was none around. This was so realistic to her that months later, when being questioned, she was able to hum the specific tune. Physicians and psychiatrists had theorized that somehow, during the operation, an area of her brain had become stimulated to activate this specific ability.

Some neurobiologists have concluded that the brain has separate subsystems for color, shape, motion and depth. I believe someday it will be established that there is also a subsystem in the brain which is stimulated into an altered state of consciousness now commonly referred to as paranormal.

At the infant stage of the soul, there is a protective, supportive energy which some perceive as a personal God. As the soul begins maturation, just like all entities in the cosmos, the maternal protective force allows infancy to advance to childhood and into young adulthood, progressing to maturity and self-propelled growth in its stride for self identity, and a mounting level of consciousness.

The soul, through this maturation tapestry, will eventually accommodate all that each day presents as an opportunity to live life fully, relishing the beauty of the earth and the miracles of the cosmos, savoring and celebrating delights, bending with the hurricanes of loss and sorrow. And, recognizing, verbalizing and demonstrating to those we love, the immeasurable joys they have heaped into our lives.

What some people call a miracle today may be an everyday occurrence explained by advanced scientific techniques fifty, or a hundred, or a thousand years later.

As we progress into the twenty-first century, I know that the extraordinary psychic will be on its way to becoming the everyday ordinary. I believe that scientists will some day discover specific brain activities during psychic activity. I believe that scientists will someday acknowledge the existence of the soul, that ongoing individual consciousness which is a microminuscule part of the large whole entity—the total universe.

A universe of no peripheries. Beyond time and space.

Questions & Answers

If you're so psychic, how come you're not filthy rich?

That's what I'd like to know!

Seriously, the type of sensitivity which those like me possess, encompasses a universal consciousness that excludes a "me" mentality, recognizing the need to play the game of life fairly, without compromises for excessive wealth.

What makes you think that your experiences are not just hallucinations?

Webster interprets *hallucination* as a "delusion"; meaning "the apparent perception, in a nervous or mental disorder, of something external that is actually not present." These psi communications occur when I'm mentally lucid, living a normal, productive life, and are followed by a waking event connected to the experience. When at times I've intentionally ignored a foreboding message wistfully relegating it to just a fluke or a "garbage" dream, later events have confirmed the experience to be a valid cosmic event.

Recently, I was talking with a young man who that morning had received a phone call telling him of his grandmother's death. In the middle of a sentence he turned pale. "You know what?" he exclaimed, "I just remembered. I had a weird dream last night. Would you believe it? Grandma and I were walking side by side when she turned to me and said, 'Son, take care of yourself.' Then suddenly she disappeared. Wow, it must've been her good-bye."

Do you think you've had more of these experiences because you have more faith than the average person?

I don't believe so. As an adult, what I've always attempted to do is to understand and analyze conclusions. What others have termed faith, I more accurately label trust. A trust that very seldom has been a blind faith of so-called invisible or supernatural forces, but an understanding that has always had to make sense to me personally, to fit in with the total nature of the universe. And, like many others, I am aware of how little Homo sapiens know and how vast a universe there is of principles and laws interacting together in ever-changing variables.

Have you never doubted?

Of course. But it's because I've doubted that I have sought; much like a scientist balancing skepticism with inquisitiveness and an open mind to new perceptions.

Why did you wait so long to write this book about your psychic experiences?

I've written since before my teens, and have been searching and keeping notes on parapsychology since young adulthood. My "ESP & You" column for the Akron Beacon Journal in 1969 was the first of its kind. And my goal in life has always been to help others.

After the death of my sister, I started keeping a journal of my psychic experiences for my own review and study. When in 1992 I retired from a full time position to work on a novel, a series of events urged me to return to my detailed journals and this book evolved.

Q&A

How come you have all this psychic ability, and we don't?

I believe that the area of the brain that harbors the sub system which activates what the human species now labels paranormal, is present in everyone. However, it appears that this zone, for a variety of reasons, as yet not completely identified, is more developed in some than in others.

Why do some appear to have more of this ability than others?

In addition to pre-existing factors, genetics, and environment, my theory is that those who have developed this ability have done so by paying more attention to their instincts, widening the path to "tuning" in to the soul of the universe.

I also believe that those who become sensitive to the cosmos are extremely sensitive to everything around them, are highly altruistic and become easily disturbed when others are in pain.

What is the down side of being psychic?

The painful sense of not being able to help, when picking up other people's hurts.

In the summer of 1992 I was troubled by a dream of an approaching devastation which would kill a great number of people. I shared my concern with Allen and Trish, comparing the ravage to that of an earthquake, but not an earthquake. It was the August 24-26 Hurricane Andrew in Florida followed by the September 11 hurricane in Western Hawaii, about which I could do nothing.

The Oklahoma City bombing on April 19, 1995, affected me as if there had been a death in my own family.

In the spring of 1996, I was planning a September trip to Paris and my agent had suggested TWA Flight 800 from New York. In the summer, I began sensing flashes of explosions.

Never having done so before (although a frequent traveler), I made a trip to the local TWA office where statistics of the Boeing 747 was outlined to me, in terms of number of engines, capacity, etc. I took home a brochure and a printout. At the beginning of July, I canceled my travel plans. On the evening of Wednesday July 17th, returning home from a line-dancing class, I switched on the TV to a screen ablaze with stunned newsmen reporting the crash of TWA 800, a Boeing 747. My flashes stopped that night.

The "kidnapping" case of the Smith boys in November 1994, was another disturbing episode in my life. I couldn't dismiss visions of water, and labored footsteps of someone pushing heavy equipment. When I heard a news flash that Susan Smith had been arrested, I knew exactly what had happened and picked up the phone to tell a startled worker at America's Most Wanted office that Susan Smith did not have any accomplices.

Do you do readings?

No.

Do you recommend that we attend psychic fairs? Or call psychic prediction centers?

If you attend psychic fairs as an adventure, without taking predictions seriously, Yes. Call psychic phone numbers? No. Save your money, or perhaps spend it on attending relaxation classes. Why? First, a serious clairvoyant does not get involved in such marketing schemes. Secondly, if the person on the other end is clairvoyant, he/she does not necessarily always pick up the auras/vibrations, and because you have paid money he/she will have to come up with some "story" (always remembering that if you're happy, you'll bring others). I know of many cases where people have been very disappointed, going into a depression, when predictions have turned out to be not true.

Have you seen any UFO's?

Once, when a friend and I were on our way to an evening meeting in Buffalo, New York, we saw a glowing large oval shaped object like a moon moving fast in the horizon. Curious, we pulled over and got out of the car just when a cigar-shaped object flew up and joined it. We watched as the two traveled together until they disappeared. It was a bright, moonlit evening and although we scouted the news for information on man-made activities that night, we found no references.

What did you think of the Heaven's Gate people's suicide in California? And are there "red lights" for those who may be thinking of joining these type of cults or religious movements?

I felt very sad for the families left behind. A red light warning would be when an organization demands that one give up all ties with family and go into isolation with the group, entirely severing previous commitments. Another alarm signal is a prerequisite that one turn over personal possessions. Most importantly, ask yourself: does the organization focus only on personal development without promoting altruistic directions for the betterment of others and the environment?

Did you get anything on what the O. J. verdict would be?

On the morning of the verdict, Tuesday, October 3, 1995, just before I woke up I had a flash of O. J. Simpson gathering his belongings from jail to go home.

When did you realize that you were psychic?

It was not so much a realization that I was psychic, as a gradual comprehension that others did not see or hear things I did. As a child I could "hear" people's thoughts, and around the age of 5, I concluded that it wasn't accepted behavior for me to tune in to other people's private feelings and thoughts, and turned it off.

Do you get precognitive dreams not relating to emotions?

Quite a few. One I shared with Allen (because he's in the computer industry), was seeing the use of an electronic gadget identifying people through various bodily characteristics, which I later learned is referred to as *Biometrics.*

Why didn't you think that the message from Jake's soul about leaving in a year-and-half, could mean that he was going to divorce you because he's found someone else?

When two people have a bond like mine and Jake's, there is always an unspoken understanding of each others' feelings. His whole demeanor, his sadness and insistence that I be sure to remember what he was saying, never reflected the possibility that it could be another woman. And I knew the advance notice was because of his concern for me.

How would I know that I've met my soul mate?

A good clue is that, sharing identical values, you generate the best in each other in a complementary relationship, where the two of you together beam brighter than the total sum of your individual parts.

You say that sometimes when there has not been a formal goodbye before death, there have been psychic experiences with the reenactment of a good-bye. Did this happen between you and Jake?

Yes. It was a sacred, private interlude.

How do you know that when you saw the baby in your dream it was your granddaughter? And how did you recognize your second granddaughter before her arrival?

Through the same instinct that animals recognize their offspring from a group of perhaps hundreds—like penguins.

I've heard of classes for relaxation and creativity training where one supposedly learns to use altered states to improve everything. How do you feel about them?

There are many good techniques one can pick up from these classes, depending on your goal. I'd caution on training techniques where you're *guaranteed* that you're going to change overnight. Some things work for others, some don't. Watch out for the ones that say exactly how many deep breaths you must take to relax. Techniques work differently for different personalities.

For relaxation and creativity I would recommend hatha yoga. Try more than one teacher to find your exact niche, for teaching techniques vary. I prefer a background of soft, soothing music capped with visualization.

Can spirituality promote health?

True spirituality promotes a sense of satisfaction which calms nerves and eases stress. Sometimes concentrating too heavily on healing without immediate positive results can increase frustration and self-blame. Go with the flow is an adage I keep in mind, balancing the physical body with spiritual mind.

Not wanting to remind a friend of a loss, most people avoid bringing up the name of the deceased. Acting as if it hasn't happened, seems kinder.

People have the mistaken notion that not talking about a person who has died, will assuage a person's loss. Bringing up the subject is showing respect for shared memories, especially by close friends. The end of the 90s will be remembered as the time death "came out of the closet."

How can I do automatic writing?

I do not advocate doing automatic writing for the purpose of simply doing it. Automatic writing should be implemented *only* in the context of seeking spiritual growth and knowledge, and only if one feels it would be the ultimate confirmation or negation of your own feelings. Also, only when one is at peace, balanced and in tune with the world focused on spiritual growth, and willing to devote a great, great deal of time in quiet meditation, relaxation, and many false starts.

If you've lost a loved one whom you **strongly feel** wants to communicate with you, sit quietly with pen or pencil in hand (or at your computer, if you wish). At first with your eyes closed, concentrate on the feelings of love, fulfillment, the unity of the universe, the joys of mundane things such as seeing the sun rise in the morning, or the chirping of the birds, or the ecstasy of the beauty of flowers. Don't attempt to move your writing implement, just let things happen.

In the beginning you will get garbage. If you get frustrated, stop. As you become more calm, the connection will be made. Practice only when body, mind and soul are in harmony. It may take weeks or months—or years of searching for spiritual balance.

Your sub-title "A time for all Seasons," would indicate that Man is a victim of predestination: That Homo sapiens do not have free will?

We do have free will to make choices, but those choices function within universal laws within specific boundaries.

What about positive thinking?

Absolutely! Positive thinking allows you to push aside undue fears, which in turn clears your thinking process. This then makes it easier to utilize whatever supportive processes are at hand. There are times when a negative attitude creates barriers; removing those barriers very often initiates a positive atmosphere that promotes a natural healing, resolution or spiritual understanding.

Don't you then believe in miracles?

I very much believe in miracles. What man has called a miracle in one century, may turn out to be an everyday occurrence which then becomes a process scientifically reinforced and taken for granted in the next century. Believing in miracles creates a can-do attitude, which in turn teaches one to be a survivor.

Whether what happens in our lives is labeled a miracle doesn't matter. What we learn from what happens in our lives, is what is essential for the evolutionary process of our soul.

What is the Kabbalah?

Simplified, Kabbalah ("Received" teachings), is a Jewish mysticism stressing the presence of Deity everywhere, outlined in story form which contain the keys to revelations in the Hebrew Bible.

What is Lucid Dreaming?

In the 1970s Dr. Stephen LaBerge developed a concept which he labeled Lucid Dreaming, identifying the process as being aware that one is dreaming. Founder and Director of the Lucidity Institute in Palo Alto, California, Dr. LaBerge works with those who believe that the dream state allows them to resolve troubling issues using devices that he has developed.

How can I determine whether my dreams are "garbage" or real guidelines?

The psi researcher is not interested in dreams which allow the working through of unconscious wishes, but in unforgettable states of consciousness that are followed by a waking experience connected to the episode.

Approach the analyses of your dreams very academically. Forgetting about past dreams, instruct yourself that from now on you will remember your dreams. If it doesn't happen immediately, continue to know that eventually (if it is important), you will.

If you wake up in the middle of, or just after, a dream, stay still, don't move around or open your eyes. Mentally, go over what just happened and recall as much as you can, then telling yourself you will remember it in the morning, relax. The next day, record everything you remember about the dream. Keeping a notepad by the bed to jot down the dream, doesn't work for me. It interferes with the mood and prevents my going back to sleep. Usually, in the morning, I jot down a few key words to jog my memory when I'm able to outline the incident in detail. Because of its ease and portability, I've often used an audio recorder, transcribing it to hard copy later.

Record your feelings: Was the dream realistic, or did it appear to be a continuation of your fears while awake? Put down colors, sensations, and items. For example, if you see water, was it clear or muddy? If there was a sky, were there clouds, or was it crystal blue? While writing it down, does another dream experience flash back which tied in with a later event? As you compute your records, a pattern will emerge highlighting the correlation of symbolic or graphic messages in your dreams, and consciousness.

In reviewing your journals, continue your academic critique to determine incidents beyond coincidences. If a pattern does not emerge, perhaps at this time in your life, you're not ready for expanded perception.

How can one tune in to the soul of the universe?

Some call it meditation. Some call it prayer. Some call it keeping the laws of their church. Some call it doing the will of God. Whatever method offers evolving constructive opportunities for spiritual anchor, increasing individual contribution to a productive, all-inclusive global harmony, is the right discipline for each person.

One very important caveat: every life on our planet Earth is precious. It is essential to remember that sometimes we, members of the human species, have also killed and plundered in the name of *God*. A graphic example is the confessed assassin of Prime Minister Yitzhak Rabin in Tel Aviv, in November 1995, who was alleged to have pronounced that he had "received instructions from God to kill the Prime Minister."

What do you recommend most for spiritual expansion?

Because so many changing variables are at work in each person's evolutionary process, different techniques become more productive at different times. First: Be wary of systems which promise immediate transformation. Second: Pursue a method that appeals to you, which does not violate another entity—including nature and the environment.

Does participation in formal religious services in a church, or synagogue, or mosque, or gathering place charge your spiritual batteries? Then follow that path. Do you feel the need for formal Bible, or Koran, or Judaic, or Hindu studies? Then answer your call. Does nature lift you up to a union with the cosmos? Then join the universe through your silence or active participation.

Your spiritual growth techniques change, as you comprehend and utilize universal energies.

Glossary

Akashic records
    Universal central depository where all one's activities are recorded. Taken from the Sanskrit *Akasha*, the ethers where all material and non-material exist in a common medium.

Astral travel
    The travel of the soul to places not bound by time or space.

Aura
    In parapsychology, the luminous atmosphere that surrounds a person, observed and understood mostly by those who are highly clairvoyant.

Automatic writing
    The process of recording a message from a source other than the person doing the recording. In psychic circles, allowing a soul who has left the physical realm to communicate in writing.

Bardo
    The states of consciousness between physical incarnations—the time from physical death until one is reborn.

Book of the Dead—Egyptian and Tibetan
    A set of literature, containing prayers and chants which assist the soul through physical death.

Book of Life
    Same as Akashic Records

Clairvoyance
    The faculty of knowing an event in advance, irrespective of time or space. Often interchanged with "psychic."

Collective Unconscious
: Psychologist Carl Jung's theory of inborn unconscious psychic material common to all mankind, accumulated by the experience of all preceding generations, available in the dream state.

Cosmic Consciousness
: The process of experiencing the unity of all things, first coined by Dr. Richard M. Bucke.

Extrasensory Perception
: Term used to denote experiences (visions, prophetic dreams, mental telepathy) that occur because of a change in that person's normal state of consciousness; or a communication received through non-identifiable sources.

ESP Cards
: A set of cards with 5 symbols (star, circle, square, cross and waves) created by J. B. Rhine in the early 30s used in pioneering ESP experimentation.

Euthanasia
: From the Greek word, meaning a painless, happy death. Usually applied in reference to bringing about a good dying.

Ganzfeld
: From the German, "whole, or uniform field." Name of labs created in the 90's engaged in controlled telepathic experimentation.

Homo sapiens
: Modern man; human being.

Karma
: The process of cause and effect: For every action there is a reaction; most often applied to compensation for everything that one does in life, whether good or bad.

Ki/Chi
: Japanese term for the life force, or spiritual energy, comparable to Western psi.

Mantra
: Originally a hymn or portion of the Hindu Veda Scriptures chanted as a prayer. More recently used to identify a specific personalized chant in meditation.

Nimbus
: A halo around a religious person; or an aura.

NDEs
: Near death experiences.

Ouija board
: A board printed with the alphabet and numbers with a pointing device used to "receive" messages from unknown or disincarnate sources. (From the French *oui*, yes, and the German *ja*, yes.)

Parapsychology
: The branch of psychology, initiated in the early 30s, and formally accepted in 1935, that investigates psychic phenomena such as: telepathy, extrasensory perception, clairvoyance, psychokinesis, etc. (Para—to denote going beyond accepted psychology).

Psi
: Spiritually based psychic energy (23rd letter in the Greek alphabet).

Psyche
: The human soul, or the mind. Most commonly used to refer to a total organism and its interaction with the environment.

Psychic
: The root meaning of the word comes from the Greek *psychikos* meaning "of the soul, spiritual."

Reincarnation
: Most popularly, the belief that one's soul will return again, after physical death, as another person. Originally a religious belief of the migration of the soul into various physical forms.

Shamanism
: Originating from the word *shaman,* indicating a priest or medicine man, generally used to refer to a healer in some North American Indian and Eskimo cultures.

Soul Records
: Same as Akashic Records.

Telepathy
: Extra-sensory communication between two minds. The word was devised by F. W. Myers in 1822 to denote the idea from one mind to another, independent of recognized channels of sense.

Vedas
: The Hindu scripture—a set of writings known as the Vedas, or "knowledge," written in the ancient Sanskrit language.

Yoga, Hatha
: The discipline of working with one's physical body through the practice of postures, incorporating stretching and breathing. In general terms, *Yoga* is the alignment of mind, body and soul through various Hindu mystical techniques.

For answers to your questions, or additional information, send a stamped, self-addressed envelope to:

Lisa Saddler
ANAIIS PRESS
P.O.Box 2143
Cupertino, CA 95015-2143